The New Testament of Business Leadership

Rod Richardson PhD, MBA

ISBN: 1-4140-0699-3 (e-book)
ISBN: 1-4140-0700-0 (Paperback)

Library of Congress Control Number: 2003097240

This book is printed on acid free paper.

Printed in the United States of America
Bloomington, IN

1stBooks – rev. 12/29/03

Table of Contents

Dedication iv

Introduction vi

Chapter One - "So you think you are a Leader..." 1

Chapter Two - Self-Analysis And Fear................................ 9

Chapter Three - 10, 9, 8, 7...Liftoff! 28

Chapter Four - Empowerment 40

Chapter Five - "Can I walk across your back, so I
can feel a little taller?" 62

Chapter Six - When Armor becomes an Anchor.............. 67

Chapter Seven - Power without Pride 79

Chapter Eight - To Bake a Cake... 86

Chapter Nine - The Christmas Story – Pieces and
Parts 120

Chapter Ten - Welcome to the Land of "Can" 129

Chapter Eleven - What Does a leader look like? 137

Chapter Twelve - "Lead...Follow...or   get   thy
worthless self behind me"! 140

Dedication

In memory of Pamela Joan Parker Fitzpatrick, a competitor, a victor,
a warrior of warriors and a blessed gift from God to all that she lovingly
empowered motivated and challenged.

She was God-given and God-removed, but her life affected
tremendous spiritual and empowering change
within countless lives.

To her memory and to the love of her life,
her daughter,
Brittany,
I dedicate this book.

Pamela Joan Parker Fitzpatrick
October 4, 1963 – November 21,2001

Introduction

At the end of the twentieth century, the shelves of bookstores were impressively stocked with "how to" books on business to-dos, and, not-to-dos, to insure, or even to guarantee success. Page after page, book after book, author after author, reaching out from the bookshelves, as a carnival barker, telling us how to, when to, who to, why to, do anything regarding the transformation of one's self, in order that we might be a successful business person; to transform yourself into an effective business, or mission leader. Publishers selling quick- read overviews of the countless "How To" books flourished, as busy executives scurried like mad men, in coffee stained shirts, folded newspapers, wrinkled suits, blood-shot eyes, attempting to carry out their required job responsibilities, yet, at the same time, stay on top of the latest epistle of business leadership.

The term, "Effective Leadership", was and continues to be, the battle cry of top executive management at every major American corporation.

In the nineties, along with the prosperity of the economic markets, a cashing-in, on every catch-phase, that was drooled, uttered, or fell out of a business leader, or CEO's mouth, also became came a paperback, a video, or a cassette tape, that spawned a seminar boosting, soliciting, urging, that if we do what they do; we will also be as successful and effective as they were, or are; rich beyond our wildest dreams, mostly due to our purchases of their books or videos.

Little was written on fulfillment, self-worth, or the contributions to our fellow man, as compared to the monetary gains and, in some cases, the artificial manipulation tactics of self-improvement. Monetary-based, personal change programs, goal setting and motivational programs, programs on leadership, pompous propaganda programs on subjects such as, LBOs, buying a business with no money down. The local bookstore was a "Reading Restaurant", were the menu, and the daily diet of the patrons, the manager struggling to succeed, was standing room only.

Interestingly, coming along at the same time as these pearls of business wisdom, came the other books, and programs, located on the next shelf; titles such as, "Get Out of Debt" programs, "Repairing Your Credit" programs, and, ultimately and understandably, mental health books and programs such as, "The Truth about Prozac", "Fighting Depression", and "Is your Family in Crisis".

This menu of delicious, available reading to the business or marketplace manager says quite a bit about the real results of some of the writings, and the results of our society in the last part of the past century, while attempting to address the ideas of leadership and contributory success.

The assault, of paper and pen, by these business prophets turned author were aimed primarily at those that called themselves, or wished to be called and/or recognized as professional salesmen, or corporate executive managers. These writers screamed for the need to read their latest "How To" book, resulting in the general business population shaming anyone that would not admit, or at the very least, lie about having read, the latest and greatest industry rage on being a successful, effective, executive leader. Pardon the sarcasm, but, let us not forget the parts about becoming filthy rich, and prosperous, by the process of reading, and applying, their instructions and behaviors.

Some of these books had great worth, some quite worth the time to read, but mostly were economic gains to the writer, who actually recorded their own lessons of life, the marketplace and their own corporate experiences. Most actually wrote of their own personal perceptions, or the life-lessons learned by the others they worked with, or studied. (I am afraid this writing also resembles some of the same)

Some of these lessons were truly valid and timely. They were lessons that withstand the test of time, and when used, and applied, in the nineties booming economy, one could question whether it was inflated economic conditions or the goldmines of empowerment.

At this point, the economic era I refer to boosted one of the greatest economic expansions in American history, certainly not the dregs of a recession, and provided and promised success at every turn, planned, earned or not.

A writer could take one idea, one truth, and expound upon the virtues of their enlightened and discovered truth, chapter after chapter, page after page, and make a significant contribution to the starving society of the hungry and challenged leaders, regardless of their rank or title.

In addressing, or reviewing these types of books, on a whole, I liken them to the Old Testament Hebrew Law. Law upon law, rule after rule, of what you had to do, to achieve your goals of pleasing God; As business laws similar to modern times, simply having your personal contributions and /or talents recognized, in order to apply your new found power, which could be utilized and given to mankind, and to the overall society, in and out of the Board Room, or the marketplace. The business commandants that were found in these books were worshipped and revered, and arrogantly pronounced, as the only way, or at the very least, putting yourself on the fast track, to achieve whatever it was you were searching for.

In the biblical days keeping the Old Testament laws as put forth by the pre-Christ writers, gave countless wisdom and teachings within the stories and the accounts of a people searching and seeking a better life; written examples of the poor souls that strayed; souls, saints and sinners that made God angry, as well as pleased. The Bible pointed out individuals, regularly, as felons of the laws of God, and graphically, spelled out and recorded His delivery of their disgrace, and punishment for their mistakes, poor decisions and sins.

It revealed stories of those that attempted to interpret the law, who fell from grace routinely, as the law became more important than the nature or intent of the Law, or the One these Old Testament laws was spiritually written by, as well as, for whom the laws were written for.

Is it that we, as humans, are like the old saying, "we can't see the forest for all of the trees". It is clear to me, and obviously to many successful, personally fulfilled business leaders that the Bible continues to represent the ultimate "How To" book on Business Leadership. When the Bible is read in fashion to be truly understood and followed, its reading becomes a life long affair to understand the wisdom of its words and its writers, and how to implement its wisdom in and out of the marketplace, or corporate environment.

However, this "Good News" of business leadership, actually represents a New Testament law regarding that of "business leadership", and the topic of leadership in general. This "New Testament" approach is different from the business books written in the past, in that it starts in your own soul, in your own relationship with Jesus Christ.

Business books rarely talk about the leader's heart, passions, fears, and moments of self-doubt, prejudices, ego, and the emotions that drive and form the outcome of their impact of their actions, or, on the very ones they lead. This book deals with the leader's heart, as well as the leader's head. It relates directly to the pure empowerment of an individual, to the team concepts and the value of a leader's own self-analysis, as well as the encouragement of the self-analysis of the individual employee and the team.

This book is not a "how to", "step-by-step", book that screams of fabulous life styles and earthly riches nor is it a bible study guide, but instead, at times written romantically, explores the depths of the leader's thoughts, passions, fears and inter-strength. It calls to those that are, "called", to the task, duty, and, unfortunately the pains of leadership. This is a fresh focus, neither on a persons' rank, nor title, but directly on a leader's inner-self, and the personal empowerment of those that follow them. It calls for honest self-examination, through deep soul-searching concepts, and realities, of the whole worth of oneself.

It addresses, at points poetically, the responsibility to those that we lead and the leaders' direct responsibility to lift up and encourage all co-workers and bosses. Leaders that are calling to all, at every opportunity, to act as a bridge, or pathway, from something old to something new, a defined mission in the leader's heart and mind, and in those that follow the leaders command.

This book's theme addresses a real change management, in the truest sense; change within one's self, and in that of empowering the change within others, that they too might reach their full God Given, designed, expectations and personal potentials.

In doing so, passing along this infectious disease called "empowerment". The trick to this book is to go slow, read slow, explore your own value and talents, and to think!

Chapter One

"So you think you are a Leader..."Leadership; I have this belief on Leadership"...

"Leaders are not anointed...they emerge from within the blood, sweat and fear of battle, not through rank or title, nor draped in arrogance or ego...but in quiet confidence, to expend the sum of their life's experience, talents, skills and God-given blessings toward the battle at hand, without regard for self, but with total regard for the success of the whole."

I have this belief on the character of a Leader. Simply said,

"Confident, not Arrogant, Humble, not Stupid" - Wayne Leistra

Could Leadership be a curse? I think not if true heart and soul are exposed! Could there be a leader that is self-centered, that deserves the toil, trust and courage of the people before, or behind him, or her?

How would it be possible to lead without the passion for pain, for self-examination, all for the payment of a pauper? Such a fine, fine line between the sadistic skill of a satanic and demeaning dictator and the heart of an empowering merchant of dreams and hope; Could there be a place between the two? I think not.

Leadership requires an eye on the possible, while struggling with feet buried in the earthly reality of lost hope, and the relentless screams of dismay and the loss of heart, while fighting and struggling to free the souls and the talents, hopes and dreams of the scattered and scorned.

A leader is deaf to claims of "can't" and reveilles in the calm of "can". Is the burden of leadership heavy? Only to the one that tries to carry "self" along for the journey!

In general, the blueprint for us and for our battles and endeavors continues to go back to Executive Trainer Richard Flynn's description for "Human Engineering". "We are designed to achieve what we are achieving; the only way to change what we are achieving, is to change the design".

The balance between the mission to be undertaken, and an absolute, clear understanding of the opposing enemy, compared to the resources at hand, coupled with the organization that is built to complement the strategy elected through personal and company self-examination, is the only recipe for success, realizing positive change and fulfillment to the fullest.

I sometimes think the misappropriation of human talent and the inability to think beyond the boundaries of our own intelligence, is the single greatest tragedy we face. It is not until you reach the battlefield, and the enemy lies before you, that the decisions we make as leaders are truly confirmed, as being right or wrong.

There has been a many of field Captain in the heat of battle, follow a Private up the hill, as the faces of his fellow fighters are frozen in fear. Often a private emerges as a leader, not in rank, but in honest valor and bravery, worried more about the overall victory and/or loss, than that of his own safety, or of any organization protocol.

However, there must always be clear, rank and file order, and organization protocol within the ranks, but not to the point that we stifle, or abuse, or waste the resources given us. As a leader, or worker, to whom much is given, much is…EXPECTED!

Vision of the possible can come from a searing, deep seeded need to survive but can also come from a competitive nature to excel beyond the others around you, while enduring their continual attempts to tear you down, and drown your enthusiasm, with words after words, of what won't work or of what you can't do. That, sadly, is the norm. This I will address later. ("Let me walk on your back, so I can feel a little taller)

True empowering, life-changing leaders are made, created from within and called to the unbelievable task of leadership, through their own inter-calling or the self realization of the things within their own heart, within their own soul; things they can not turn away from.

"For We Are Made"

It is what it is,

an explosion of struggle

an infinite number of options,

all bearing the dregs,

the depths

of dismal failure,

one to another,

taunted by a screaming demand

for action

direct,

deliberate,

painful action

without hesitation,

or concern

for things

in the balance of the heart,

for the action of leadership,

to save the things

that generations

beyond us,

count upon,

even now,

as we,

as leaders,

and they,

as our followers,

require us

to suffer through,

expose and exploit,

dominate and defend,

cradle and conquer,

that we all might exist.

Leadership,

real leadership

that of generals

on the field of battle,

requires much.

Things that are bestowed

not earned,

granted from God,

yet,

can only be obtained

through the blood of battle

and the swing of a sword,

and the love of heart

and the compassion of soul,

to fight for all,

including self,

so that self may be given

to,

and for,

another.

God bless the battle
And the fruits thereof.

Hello, is there anybody out there?

You have heard it before, 'it's lonely at the top". When thinking and dealing with the horrible, frightening feelings of being alone as a leader, the lyrics of an old country song, sung by Kathy Mattea, seems to always come to my mind, "standing knee deep in a river, and drowning of thirst". The demands of leadership in battle screams for self-examination, without the luxury of confirmation, and without recognition of a leader's own personal struggle. This is a leader's struggle to honestly look at our own inadequacies as it relates to our leadership skills and the outcome of the battle at hand.

There is no "Alone" in the world, lonelier than that of a true leader - particularly, while trying not to get in the way of the talented people surrounding them, or the misappropriating the financial and physical resources that a leader is generally given to win the war, or in some cases, "just to take the hill".

Is a leader some super human that understands, and actively employs true guidance and direction to his followers, while being bombarded with enormous options, that can spell victory or defeat? I think not.

We all breath the same air, we all get to this earthly field of battle the same way. We are all trying to survive and to make a living. The difference between those called to lead and those called to follow, is the desire to completely expend the total sum of one's life and talents, for a brief, yet brilliant moment of service, all to be sacrificed for the success of the whole, without typical, earthly, regard for self.

The difference between an empowering leader, one that is a visionary and an opportunist, to that of a traditional, status quo business leader, one that clones others are incredibly apparent, and definable, to the hungry and the lost.

Those who follow the merchant of dreams are the lost, as they look for hope. Those that follow the self-centered and arrogant, are the scared and hopeless, which do so from fear, scared of change, scared of failure and petrified of self analysis".

Chapter Two

Self-Analysis And Fear

To look in the mirror and notice the changes made within your own face, from life itself, is the first step to recognizing change, and in some of our cases, the need thereof. To stand still, without change, is to die.

You have heard the expression, "Don't Fix, What Ain't Broke". If a mission of leadership does not require and invite, even demand, absolute personal analysis then arrogance, and the pride of title, or personal prestige, has surpassed humility, rendering a leader to the dregs of defeat.

To appraise something is to doubt its worth, its content, and its ability to be better than it was before. The act of appraising oneself, or seeking the meaning of oneself, or one self's source of being, talents and power, must be individually undertaken and faced. This solitary act must be done before one can empower others, and introduce others to their own strengths and talents.

Doubt leads to investigation, investigation leads to confirmation, and confirmation leads to confidence, not arrogance. Confirmation of self, or realization of self, must take place, before the value of self can be appraised, judged, changed, and honestly presented and represented, and conclusively, given to another. Self-analysis must occur before one can realize the enormous depth, strength, joy and pain of leadership itself.

To stand before oneself in the heat of honest humility, in self-analysis, is to purge the fires of self–glorification, arrogance and pride. To review one's own worth is truly humbling when one comes face to face with the flaws of one's own character and the horrific history of one's own mistakes. The temptation to see what one wants to see and wants to believe, is the foundation of disempowerment, and the dilution of the God–given powers at hand for self and for others. This power will, and can, effect enormous change in the lives of others, and above all, positive changes within you.

The courage required to submit oneself to such painful scrutiny of self-analysis is without earthly comparison. The battle to honestly review what you are made of is to place oneself in the line of direct, unforgiving fire of self-analysis; an act that evokes, naturally, the temptation to submit to the cowardly act of self-flight from yourself. A process that more than not, encourages the creation of alibis, or justifications for past actions. The guaranteed pain within this process, unleashes fruits of character, all derived from this personal battle. They are beyond imagination, or earthly comparison. This battle of self magically presents the power to free those in bondage around you, locked away in their self-imposed prisons, be it the denial of their god-given gifts, or their lack of self-esteem. It can positively embrace all of the trials, mistakes and joys of your life, unto this meaningful, wise and powerful end – that of a true leader.

To have control and to impose this awesome power is to be a merchant of dreams, and of hope, and of sweet life itself. To contribute to mankind, by your own actions, through the analysis of self, accepting and implementing change where needed, allows self to be given freely, and without pretense, or pride.

As was said earlier, "Confidence, not Arrogance, Humble, but not Stupid'.

In biblical times, a people known as the Edomites built a city by carving it into rock. It is to this day known as a must-see tourist attraction. However, the Edomite's pride in their city was counted and judged by a declaration and judgment from God, "Though you soar like the eagle, and make your nest in the stars, from there I will bring you down, declares the Lord" (Obadiah 1:4)

They had great security in their architectural accomplishments, as their City of Petra, carved in rock, through meticulous painstaking efforts and labors, also were the source of their pride and boasting of their accomplishments. Petra fell to its destruction and ruin, as will the proud.

Through humility in self-analysis, one can find a much more accurate perception of self and our contribution to the world than what we are conditioned to believe, by our egos, or lack of it, and the opinion of the world.

In the book of Proverbs 16:18-19 it is clearly recorded, "Pride goes before destruction, a haughty spirit before a fall, better to be lowly in spirit and among the oppressed than to share plunder with the proud".

It is more important to recognize what you feel, than it is of what you think. Instead of asking a child what he is truly thinking about ask them what they feel.

The language of thought and intellect is of the mind; the language of the heart is what you feel, the conscience is the very place where God, has placed your gifts and talents. Heavenly gifts placed within you by and through the Holy Spirit; Gifts that God Himself has bestowed upon you. Godly powerful gifts, free to use, explore, enjoy and share; gifts to openly and honestly share with each other. Gifts once recognized and embraced through self-analysis, that can be put into action through the empowerment of others.

The heart or the conscience is also the very place where fear invades, with a horde of demons, to deny the self-recognition of your worth to yourself, and to your fellow man. "For everyone that asks, receives; he who seeks, finds; and to him who knocks, the door will be opened"

(Matthew 7:8). For my writings, or any others for that matter, are of little merit or worth, when considering the instruction of self-analysis placed forth in the Bible.

Seek of yourself passionately, who you are, what you have become by the world's standards, and then by the fruits of the gifts, given to you by the One that made you.

This metamorphosing, magical wand is of self-analysis will allow you to find the empowerment that can be embraced, and passed on to those around you, and to those that you led. Through this review of self you will find the freedom to be the real you and the power to free those around you. Co-workers and colleagues that are held hostage, restrained and held captive, in their own world of imprisonment; held in a jail made of from their own self-defeating disease; a disease fed by the lack of self worth, the lack of self-esteem, and the lack of recognition of the everyday gifts that God has bestowed upon you.

It is amazing what one can see when looking in the mirror with honest intent, even if just shaving or brushing your teeth. I discovered "self" at this type of moment; seeing myself in the bathroom mirror; an experience that fed the words of the following writing, "Will I Ever Know".

This process requires courage, (not shaving, but self analysis) and lots of it to stay the course of one's self-analysis. The pain is sometimes so great. The mere thought of such an honest appraisal, leads one to run petrified, in complete terror, creating any thought, or lie, to subdue the sting of the very view before them.

But this sometimes, not so gentle push to this place of evaluation, or disgrace, must sooner or later be faced, as the heart constantly calls to you from within. Through guilt or glory, one must make the trip of self-evaluation, to set up the playing field for making real changes, yielding real contributions within your own life, as well as changes within others.

"*Will I Ever Know?*"

The lines in his face

tracing the sorrows

of deep memorable pain,

yet also marked the delightful,

curious carvings,

eloquently etched,

from the joys of unbridled laughter,

told much more

than the stories told of a life,

spent as a man

of trial and triumph.

Yet, his eyes

ran blue of ice water,

with an intensity of purpose

that would make

a blazing fire seem tame.

From where,

was this face

of this heart made?

What could create

such a contradiction?

Was it the grief

from the tolls and task

of battles past,

or simply,

the delight of a child,

with complete trust,

the honesty

of unconditional love;

a love

that transcended

the betrayals of man,

betrayals

even by that of a fellow man,

maybe

even one he fought for.

Maybe this face was born

from a hope

that God's people

were above the petty,

above the scorn

of the hateful,

the judgments

of the jealous,

the methodical and meticulously cruel,

the infecting sickness

of a people

lost to themselves,

without regard,

without compassion,

for the hearts

and the pains of others.

What has this face seen
that seems to have surpassed
the heavenly heights of love,
yet lives below the depths
of a doomed
and dismal darkness?

What tranquil,
yet torrid transformation
could possibly
paint this face of wisdom,
and yet,
portray
that of a passionate longing
to be understood,
and loved,
yet remaining in the silent
and somber shadows,
to serve as a slave,

without arrogance or expectations,

locked in a house of hope,

not for himself,

but for the release of others,

ones that bravely battle daily

to be freed.

Such a darkness,

yet such a brilliant light,

that charismatically

cast itself

upon the dreams of others,

to guide the way,

to a place

where true self is realized,

and dreams are real as is the day

to the morning born.

Dreams that were carved

in the joyous faces

of all that dared

to believe in themselves,

just because this face did.

Monumental undertakings

that were made to seem so normal,

as the waking to a new

and glorious,

bursting day of hope

and predestined purpose.

A face that seemed to quietly scream

with a deafening defiance,

to those who would dictate doom;

A face that insured

and proclaimed,

your dreams are at hand,

seize them,

for they are within your grasp.

In this face...

so dark; yet,

so boldly bright.

Could those lines that I see,

be the painting

of a pure and perfect heart,

beating for a chance

to redeem

the horrors

of a romantically,

wasted and tormented life,

my own?;

a life that could never find

the release

from its' own infinite passion.

A soaring,

yet captured spirit,

caught in a place

that would never

compassionately

grant

such a flawless flow

of complete selfless expression.

Will I ever know?

Will I ever understand?

Perhaps not.

In a short and brief moment,

the flood of a thousand rivers

cascade over a place

that is laid so bare

to human touch and sight,

yet

in this faces' past,

no one sees,

no one feels,

for as the norm,

one rarely goes

to the places of the heart

and of the soul,

for in most of us

miserable mortals,

the pain is too great.

The fear of self

stifles us

to face our personal pains,

to get to the summit

of self-realization,

to our field of gold.

A field

that is so free

to love within,

and to abundantly give,

and to serve

and to submit,

and to express the thoughts

and the purely

delicate passions,

of true unmistakable,

undeniable love.

Are these lines in this face a place to hide,

or are they a place to explore?;

to uncover the soulful

and sweet surrender of self

and selfishness,

a place that one can fall

so helplessly complete,

to the truth of ones' own heart.

What an incredible,

exhausting journey

this face

must have made,

and must still make.

An eternal search,

not seeking its' salvation

by struggle,

but by a simple,

sweet

and selective surrender,

to its' own heart,

beating,

begging

for forgiveness,

redemption,

the chance to love

beyond earthly terms,

and above all,

to eternally embrace

its' own peace

through purpose.

Who made this face?

Will I ever know,

perhaps not?

But,

in this face,

I will forever feel.

Before one realizes he, or she, is called to Leadership, life has an ultimate demand, to survive and make a living, while constantly being placed in situations that demand, through your own inter feelings, to fit in, to blend in, if only for the feeling of security, or comfort, to be like everyone else. They call it being normal. At the very least, you try to feel like you are normal.

However, as a soldier in a war, one must know how to follow, before one can know, or appreciate, how to lead. As self-analysis is made during the battle, one is elevated to the inter-calls of leadership, whether the leadership is of one to another, or merely mustering the courage to fight the battle in the first place.

In the heat of battle, one can become unconscious of their actions of leadership. Suddenly they realize, they are an example to those around them, people that secretly watch them as an example to follow, such as a senior or street-smart person, without a need for their own personal recognition, though maturity and life's battles manifests them through life's lessons, as leaders.

When realizing a leadership role, as well as the audience before them, an over-whelming sense of courage and fear, pride and humility, decision and indecision, strategy and reckless abandon, worth and worthlessness, invades the leader's mind. In most cases, this awakening brings the leader to their knees, shaken to the very core of their being.

The fear is real, the self-doubts are demonic, and the feelings of inferiority within one's own self are real. To face this fear requires pure courage and sometimes, reckless abandon to combat a leader's indecision and more than not, the popular, standard approved, normality.

Using Christ as an example, He had complete and total reckless abandon to what people thought of Him. He answered the call from His father. Christ had a choice as the Father gives us one. The defining moment to face one's inter-calling to leadership is without measure, especially when placing oneself in an unforgiving life of service and placing one's personal ego aside as well as your regrets.

Reliving time after time, moment after moment, the temptations of the act of flight, through the pure cowardice to face the depth of one's own character, and the installed, or commanded duties of a leader, only heightens the fears of leadership, and the responsibilities thereof. Standing among the warriors beneath, or beside you, awaiting the start and the outcome of the battle at hand, awaiting the results of your efforts, your preparations; all of which creates your inner emotions and anxieties are without proportion. To face the battle is one thing, but to face your own fear and self-doubt is horrendous.

Chapter Three

10, 9, 8, 7…Liftoff!

At one time in my life, I trained commercial grade ranch horses. As part of my duties owning and operating a working quarter horse training center of these well-respected equine partners of the working and competing American cowboy, my job was to start young horses. The word "old cowboys" used to use was to "break" a young horse; until the modern day trainer decided he didn't want to break something that wasn't broke. God sent the horse to earth, with all the functions, characteristics and talents the horse needed to be horse. Besides it took so much more time to fix what wasn't broke to begin with.

I started two year old quarter horses on their path of learning to become what God had fashioned them to be. The quarter horse is physically built to be agile, quick, calm and powerful, genetically proportioned, to discharge the equine duties of a four-legged friend and to be a partner to the working and competitive cowboy. A partnership that was the cowboy's life's blood on the ranches and in the rodeo sports arenas in America. Rodeo, a competing, fast-growing sport, has become a livelihood for some; a sport that is tough, yet for its participants it is a wonderfully, romantic obsession, that represents a working partnership between man and horse. Being a cowboy is an occupation, and an equine partnership that is to this day required in the feedlots and the vast commercial cattle operations; Being a Rodeo cowboy is an absolute obsession, which is a separate book within itself.

When introducing oneself as a trainer to a scared and frightened two-year old stud colt or filly, a trainer must address the horse's fear, and their natural flight response that God sent them here with. When the untrusting, wary equine student is introduced to a sixty foot round pen, with eight foot walls, without a halter or a rope attached which a human might attempt to control the animal physically (ha-ha), the sixty foot circle represents the horse's entire world. This pen becomes confining world they cannot escape, made of a wall they cannot jump, nor does it possess a corner in which they can hide their face or pretend to ignore their fear, or perceived danger.

Initially, when brought into the pen, most search frantically, seeking a place they can position and/or align their bodies in such a way as being very still and hiding their face in a corner, so as to articulate their powerful and accurate kick at the source of danger, the trainer; A kick that which most certainly, if connected fully, would render their enemy a devastating blow, and hence eliminate the perceived danger to the horse. The horse's other reaction is to run, looking outside the pen, seeking an escape route to flee, known as the horse's natural defense mechanism, the "Flight Response".

A horse's God-given response to danger is to run, and flee from danger. Even though born in captivity, and raised by loving, carrying humans, the horse's God-given response is the same in captivity, as it is in the wild. The horse's God-given defense mechanism is not to fight, but is to run, with great speed, at the first indication of imposed, or impending danger. However, the circle of the pen quickly becomes a horrifying experience, as they attempt to flee danger, running in a circle, yet never being able to escape.

The mere existence of a human, within a confined environment, in which they cannot escape, evokes the flight response and magnifies the horse's fear. The horse runs, dodges, darts racing around the pen looking for anyway out of his captivity, and his predicament. This is an honest response to the natural design of a horse; a response designed by God, and which represents the honesty of a horse.

In short, they will honestly kick your head off if denied the use of their God-given response to danger.

As we humans respond to fear, we also feel the instinct, to choose the path of the horse, and attempt to, or at least think about, running as a natural response to peril and danger. Sadly, yet as is humanly normal, we sometimes choose to fight, in some cases due to pride or arrogance, or from the embarrassment of appearing as a coward in the mist of our comrades or peers; or possibly actually acknowledging, and making public, our fear.

Unfortunately, most times we choose to fight for the wrong reason. More often than not, we do not possess the courage to face the battle of unveiling the character of our self, to our self. We tend to see all that stands in our way, or things that separate us from completing our defined mission, even those things required for our mere existence, as the enemy. Instead, we need to face the enemy that lies within us first – our fear and our own lack of self worth and the recognition of the worth of others.

During each initial lesson the horse relies on his instinct, a God given instinct to run. In some cases they run, and run, and run, almost to pure exhaustion, within the circle against the wall of the pen, looking outside the pen, attempting to flee, find a place to flee, but to no avail. They are doing what is natural, attempting, to put distance between them and their assumed danger represented by the human that stands silently in the middle of the circle.

The human, or trainer, is not doing anything to provoke the horse, but is merely standing there, without motion; except to keep his body and his face poised toward the horse as they run continuously in a circle, while the horse continues to look for a way out, or for a place to escape their perceived danger. With humans, as well as the horse, "perception is reality".

One of the first lessons the trainer must teach the horse is to face their fear, not run from it; a notion that is completely opposite of what the horse, instinctively, is born to do.

The technique is simple; make it hard to do the wrong thing, but easy to do the right thing. Tell the horse what he is doing right, by your actions, more than telling him, through your actions, what they are doing wrong. As the trainer stands in one spot, in the absolute middle of the pen and in the furthest position from the horse, only facing the frightened horse as he runs the circle against the wall. The horse will tire of his attempted flight and finally stops, either through sheer exhaustion or from realizing there is no way out.

As humans, our body, through a sense of self-survival, tells us when to stop and rest. Although for the horse, similar to humans, fear can push them past this point of logic, and they will run to their own physical damage ignoring their instinctive sense to listen to their own body and stop and rest. The trainer must be careful of the strong willed horses as they can harm themselves through an overly sensitive desire to respond to their instinctive flight-response nature, stopping at nothing to escape.

As in most cases, the horse stops for rest, they will cut their eye toward the source of their fear. When the horse cuts his eye toward the trainer even for split second, the trainer immediately takes a step backward, taking his pressure of the trainer's presence off of the horse, rewarding the horse for their brief glance toward the trainer (the horse just looked at their own fear for the first time). The horse, still untrusting, turns or looks away, dictating an action for the trainer to take one-step forward toward the horse, replacing the pressure placed upon the horse by the trainer's presence, his original, central, middle of the pen, stationary position.

Each time this happens, the trainer judges the length of the glance and moves backward and forward, in direct proportion to the movements and actions of the horse, and relative to the horse's position and speed, both, as compared to the trainer's position to the horse within the pen.

The horse realizes that when he faces the trainer, or his fear, they can control, or push their fear away from them at their will. Soon the horse is turning his head, not just an eye, toward the trainer, (again, toward their fear, represented as the trainer), they look at their object of fear, directly, longer and longer, now using their body attempting to push the trainer away, at the horse's will, by their actions upon the trainer.

Horses learn through repetition. As the trainer becomes slower to give the reward of distance, based on the amount of distance from and to the horse, the horse soon learns to push harder, turning quicker, to push the trainer away quicker; learning how to face their fear and gain positive results.

The horse has now learned that turning his entire body to the trainer, in order to move the trainer away from him and attempting to control his environment and the presence of danger, the horse has actually learned what the trainer set out to teach them to begin with, to face their fear, and learn from "pressure and release", as it is called these days. (Making it easy to do the right thing, hard to do the wrong thing)

As the horse is now facing the trainer straight ahead, body directly in line and straight ahead at the trainer, the trainer starts to move in a lateral position, to the horse's position. This action by the trainer results in moving the horse's entire body right and left, at the trainer's will, in relation to the position of the trainer in the pen, as the horse attempts to keep danger at bay, applying what the horse has learned by using their body.

As the trainer moves right and left, and works to a position that the trainer can actually walk behind the horse, it forces the horse to turn completely around, so as to keep his face on the trainer, attempting to apply what he has learned to keep danger away from them; but in fact, it has brought the horse closer, kind of like reverse psychology. The result is be able to turn your back to the horse, the trainer walking away, and subsequently, the horse, by following the trainer, like a puppy dog, trying to keep his position in relation to where the trainer is in the pen, following the trainers every step, remembering the closer he can stay to this human, the more control he has over his perception of danger. The horse now understands he has a positive action to use against they fear, and uses it to control their environment.

By the horse facing their fear, they have learned to control, and overcome their fear by learning how to respond through the trainer's actions. The closer they are to the trainer, the more they are in control, and the more they can relieve themselves of the instinctive response to fear - fright and flight.

I have always said it is hard to find a good horse trainer that does not, at the very least, understand the principals of Christianity. The closer you get to the Master, the better off you are.

At this point, the horse has conquered their fear by having control, not over the object of their fear, but over their own natural response, to their own instinctive response, to the things they do not understand, or the things that are represented as harmful, or scary, due to their lack of understanding, or a new direction in their life.

The horse has learned, not through the struggle against his natural response to fear, but through the submission to the understanding of the effects that fear has upon them, they embrace their ability to have total control over their fear, controlling their outcome, through their submission, and their direct courage to take a proactive position, by doing what is rewarded, doing pro-active things, applied by their actions instinctively.

This is very similar to the bible teachings, that you find salvation through surrender, not through struggle. I say again, you will never, truly find a "real" horse trainer, that doesn't fully understand the principles of Christianity.

As in humans, we must learn to face our fear. I assure you, when settling down in the saddle of an untrained, or as they say an "unbroken" horse, I assure you, you face your fear.

As the handlers release the horse and it becomes just you and the horse, alone in the middle of the pen, horse and rider, succumbing to facing each other's fear, but mostly facing your own, it is at that moment that your instinctive nature of self-preservation arises and your own "Flight Response" kicks in. In the case of us humans, the "Flight response" is asking yourself how high I will fly when this horse bucks me off.

Knowing that you are now subject to the violent, physical movements of the horse's reaction to fear, then your own fear erupts; you realize that you can get bucked off or as old cowboys say," you can elect to leave". This is an old cowboy term that indicates you choose to bail out or jump as opposed to facing the dirt at a velocity that is less than friendly.

However, it is now up to you to rely on your seat in the saddle, being able to stay on, and use a parental, compassionate spur, to correct the horse's misbehavior, by making it "hard to do the wrong thing, and easy to do the right thing".

There is a that millisecond that you can feel the horse react to their fear, their muscles tense up and they poise and posture their bodies preparing to throw you into next week and naturally, get rid of this foreign object on their back - you and the saddle. Imagine, a "Horse-tronaut", launched, without the rocket., wearing boots, cowboy hat and spurs.

When you settle down in the seat of the saddle, you feel like the weight of all time lies upon your shoulders. You are forced by your mere existence to face your fear and rely on your ability, or stupidity, to stay in the saddle and hopefully, on top of the horse. You must spur the horse in a corrective manner, as they act up, or buck, or you can elect, through your own fear, to try and be as still possible, hoping that they will behave, not buck, pitch, roll or fall. As far as the horse being still and behaving almost never, never, ever happens.

This defining moment of facing your fear and correcting your pupil's behavior is using your spurs to scold and correct them in a parental fashion. You can decide not to spur, try and sit there; still and silent, hoping for the best, hoping that they do not buck, or hurt you. This approach of sitting as still as a statue, most always ends up, historically, as a wreck. You are defeated; cause you have not fully addressed the inevitable; the fact that the horse's natural instinct is to buck you off, not due to anger, but due to fear.

To face your fear at that moment of decision, to spur or not to spur, to correct or not to correct, is the same instinctive reaction we face when the monumental challenges of our lives, that we as leaders, parents, employees face, when we find ourselves in unfamiliar territory; doing things differently, things that stand before us that are not familiar. It is as simple as the difficulty of dealing with the things we don't understand, or just facing fear itself, regardless being the fear's cause, or it's catalyst.

As the horse's natural response to fear is to run, we, as humans are similar to the horse, we must overcome fear through self-analysis, and facing our fear, finding consistent control and victory over our predicament. The joy to know one's self, and the confidence of knowing that you have the courage to face one's self and life's predicaments, is a wonderfully life-enriching experience. It will stay with you until the end of your time.

The radiance and joy of self-confidence is without measure, and the glow of humility is blinding to the proud and arrogant, as they stand defeated before you. The power of change, by and through the empowerment of others, and the art of changing yourself, is at your beckoned call. It is a on-call "Crown of Victory", a glorious weapon on demand 24 hours a day, 7 days a week, 365 days a year, at your will, to prevail, to succeed, to win.

Being fearless is not an act of stupidity; it is an opportunity to manipulate the crippling emotion of fear, into direct, positive, predetermined action; knowing how to face your own fear, and helping those around you face theirs.

Chapter Four

Empowerment

As leaders of men and women, we are put in a position, as a bridge between the old and the new, the past and the future. To cast your self as a vehicle, a bridge, that allows a person to move between mediocrity and excellence in having a job, verses that of a livelihood, we sometimes fail to realize that our boundaries can become that of another's, if we ask a subordinate to do as we would do, or think as we would think, never allowing ourselves to be enlightened by a subordinates abilities, talents or intellect; never allowing ourselves, in the leader's role, to think beyond our own intelligence, and embrace the skills and the talents of others to contribute to the defined mission and the victory at hand.

The key to empowerment is to create an environment that allows people to be whom God created them to be. The arrogance of believing, that we, as leaders; have all the answers and all the solutions is the greatest form of self-glorification and stupidity. It is the very sword your enemies seek to defeat you, a weapon that can destroy you completely, from within, without your enemy ever having to draw or raise their blade against you.

To empower is to become powerful. To respect and embrace your own power is to become victorious. As leaders we must accept our role as a

"Bridge" to those we lead and those that do not understand they need to be led. We must permit passage without prejudice, without judgment, based not upon our own intelligence and personal recognition, or the lack thereof, but directly upon the desires, dreams, and the drive of the traveler and their God-given gifts. Those that travel across this bridge are our subordinates and followers, those that call us "Boss".

It is a leader's duty to make available the path from the old to the new while recording the journey, the pain, the promise, the plans and the hopes of each who crosses the bridge the leader creates. The leader must attempt to build a bridge that point in the direction to the ultimate destination of victory, regardless where the traveler's journeys began, or will ultimately lead to. An empowered leader is an experienced bridge builder.

"The Bridge"

To silently stand before

the old wood and steel bridge,

depressingly draped

in the wet, gray moss,

as mother nature

takes back her own,

worn from the loads of time

and travelers,

it was easy to feel

the toil of the hopeful,

wishing to find

a conscience connection

between where they had been,

and where they were going.

A stark and once sturdy reminder

of dreams,

from past glorious undertakings,

that still stood

as a monument,

to the courage,

and the hope

of the souls,

hearts and minds

that built them,

forever striving

to get from

one place to another.

Either traveling

from a place of pain

seeking deliverance,

or in a methodical march,

seeking the shear joy of adventure,

constantly seeking

a purposeful,

meaningful use of themselves,

while searching soulfully

for what the world had to offer.

I am frozen to ponder,

and to think deeply,

of what people saw

as they approached

this time worn and withered bridge,

or what they saw

when the bridge was born,

when it was new

to the divide it crossed.

With every step,

creak

and bending board,

did they wonder,

would it hold their weight,

or did they

have the blinded assumption

that it was sturdy as stone,

all while making decisive steps,

without giving a thought

to the hands and hearts

that built it,

or what they would do

without its' back to walk upon,

to solemnly stand

as a selfless servant,

to the mission of dreams.

I think of the power

and the joy,

as the bridge felt

each heart and hope,

through the souls of a worn out shoe

looking for a better life,

the hoof of a horse

and the burden it pulled or carried,

and the joys of a child playing on it rails,

leaping into the air,

to be gloriously submerged

in to a vast, wet and wonderful

peaceful river below.

A bridge somehow represents

change from the old

to the new,

a passage

from one time to another,

from pain to power,

from sadness to joy,

from lost hope to renewed spirit

of heart and health.

A bridge,

simple its not.

If considering the truth of a bridge,

it connects the pains

and lessons from the past,

to the hope and promise of tomorrow,

of a delivered spirit

being reborn,

renewed,

and simply rewarded

for the journey itself.

Did the architects fully realize

the empowerment

their structure represented?

The magic door to a future,

to a new life,

built on the foundation

of human need

to advance

and to move beyond yesterday.

Knowing,

that to stay still,

without the journey of life,

was to die.

Oh the noble servant the bridge is,

to stand alone,

without praise or payment,

to wait for,

in solitude,

and to be charged with the joy to serve,

to test its strength under the load,

a load possibly

never felt,

yet forever to be felt.

To stand in quiet, sturdy confidence,

that it will,

and can,

bear the load.

To boldly buckle and creak,

and bend from the weight,

yet

support the weight

of the heaviness of a heart,

or the spirit

from the travelers seeking to cross.

To bear the weight of the fear

of those going in the unknown,

and to freely grant passage

to the hope of a people struggling

to go forward into the future.

The hopeful never look back

while crossing the bridge,

for the first step

is the commitment to succeed;

For at that first step

they start their passage,

to succeed,

yet for the weak and doomed,

those that fear change,

the first step represents

a opportunity to fall,

to fail,

be it their first step

or their tenth,

eminent death is the same.

I have never seen a horse,

for whatever reason they cross,

look backwards

when crossing a bridge;

their eyes are on the end of the bridge,

the other side.

Oh,

but there are those

of the human nature

that look over the side,

not to enjoy the view,

but as to decide,

or imagine,

how they will be destroyed

if,

or when,

the bridge will give way,

without self worth or personal confidence,

looking to be given

the perfect alibi for their failure,

and, of course,

through no fault of their own,

as if it even matters,

they will fall,

or as in the real world,

fail.

But to the bridge's mind,

and to mine,

they might as well jump,

for they have already planned

for their failure,

predestined their dishonest journey

and look for opportunities

to doom the journey

of all that go in the direction of change.

I wonder if the bridge ever says,

"Jump,

you are not worthy of my pain,

my support,

my guidance

from old to new.

If you don't die here,

you will die

from fear

and a self-centered existence

of dismal failure later,

and worse yet,

present yourself

as a stumbling block

for a young and hopeful heart

joyously racing

to find the glorious

and personal victory

of God-given gains and gifts,

to make a human contributions".

Yet a bridge,

without the prejudice

for the quality of man,

lets all pass,

without credentials,

without the power of intervention,

without the lungs or mouth

to warn the hopeful,

or the scared of heart,

of the dishonest travelers

among them.

Oh for the solemn respect

I have for this bridge,

to hold secretly the innocent footprints

of the hopeful

and to withstand

the weight of the worthless.

It is no accident that a person seeks

the bridge to jump from;

to face his,

or her self- decided doom.

He or she

could do as much damage

to themselves

by climbing a tree

and jumping to their death,

or climbing a mountain

to throw their miserable

and lost souls

from its peaks.

Yet,

they choose the bridge,

to commit their self-destruction;

Such a wonderfully

poetic place for death,

a place between the hope of the future

and the pain of the past.

Frozen,

paralyzed

and dis-empowered,

unable by choice,

to go forward,

broken and empty,

pronounced dead from holding on,

by staying in the past,

worse yet,

standing in the middle,

stopped,

dead and cold,

plunging themselves in a self indictment

of pure and absolute failure,

over the bridges side.

What a just

and righteous place

for the death of a heart,

frozen in fear,

without the courage

to arise and face life

for it splendor of change,

and the promise

of tomorrow's worth.

To all the bridges we face in life,

I humbly

and respectfully submit

my complete appreciation

to your solemn,

quite

and dedicated duty;

To stand,

to support,

without complaint

the weight of the worthy

as well as the weak,

to cross your noble and silent frame.

As the leader, are you the bridge; or are you the empty void, the vast wasteland that separates the lost from the found, the living from the dead, and the brilliantly successful from the dismal failures? Are you the noble structure that exist between something old and something new, between hope and disempowerment, the missing connection between a livelihood and a job; or are you the anchor that grounds, or drowns the human spirit's natural will to survive, to flourish, to succeed?

To fully embrace your ability to lead and to become the bridge, is to confirm what is right within yourself, what is right that stands right before, or behind you, more than proclaiming some self-righteous judgment, or pointing out what is wrong with all that is in your vision.

Make it an absolute point, as you lead, to tell your followers what they are doing right, far more than what they are doing wrong. Do not make "right things" up, creating false praise, nor constantly praising them, in that your praise will become diluted, and resented. Diligently seek the things you employees or co-workers are doing right, adding to the worth of the whole. People are more apt to emulate the behavior of doing things right when told of them, rather than dwelling on the things they have been scolded for. Remember, make it easy to do the right thing and hard to do the wrong thing. You are the trainer, the teacher, act, no...don't act, behave like one.

Set the boundaries between right and wrong by encouraging the self worth of another, by and through their own actions. To empower, is to assist, to serve, as a servant, to be the bridge, to be the one that can conduct and encourage the behaviors of all, regardless, to a glorious, victorious end.

To be placed in a leadership position is to serve those that follow you, not be served, as some would think. To become the highest, or the most powerful, one must learn to serve, to become the lowest; to empower those around you to be more than you can be; yet allowing the fact of everyone being different, by design, in thoughts or actions.

Each individual has a unique set of talents and gifts that have been given them. If all your followers, or subordinates do is perform to your own ability, you never allow them to find their own excellence, nor are you ever rewarded with the talents that you, yourself, do not possess. If this resembles your approach to being in charge, you will never find the rich and meaningful rewards of leadership, nor will the contributions you strive to give be felt.

It is an old business adage that you should surround yourself with those smarter than yourself. Look at the U.S. Presidents that have employed this tactic. Their success in leadership was unparalleled. However, if through your pointing out all the wrong things, constantly to those beneath you, they will only perform to the level of your own intelligence, or criticisms and will only act based upon the gifts, or understandings, that you have been given, never discovering the talents and gifts of their own.

Never get mad, or angry, at the subordinates actions, until you first define the situation that caused the behavior to begin with. Doing this can be easy, yet at the same time, is sometimes very hard, for it begins with, and through, the act of self-analysis. Put yourself in their shoes, if you can, if you have the courage to try. That is a key to a compassionate approach to team building, change management and true leadership.

This act of leadership requires for you to think beyond your own intelligence. More times than not, it is you, the leader which has made the mistake, by putting the wrong person in the wrong job; or your business, or industry practices has created a situation that abuses the very people you fight to empower and lead.

A weak leader manages by heavy-handed management styles, or creates a management style, driven by the implementation of their own low-self esteem. Some managers need to feed their ego regularly. They are apt to divert the real reason for poor performance upon those beneath them, instead of taking the reasons, or results unto themselves. This destructive demon, called ego, yields arrogance and is the opposite of the positive side of the "can do attitude", called "pure confidence in self", confidence in the team, and in the value of the mission itself.

Embrace a management style that is respectful of rank and title, but not to the point of being paralyzed by creating a scornful environment just because someone has a new thought. This will create a paranoid environment where employees fear the very leaders they follow.

You have arrived when your subordinates interchange ideas with you freely, without having a fear of being put down, rejected without even hearing or understanding their concerns or viewpoints, when they don't fear trying something new and instinctively tell you about it before they try it, as a child would, when a child finds a way to make their parents proud of them for their new and inventive actions to solve a problem that affects them, their parents or the entire family. When your team, individually and collectively, seeks to make you proud of their God-given ability to use their brain and their evolvement to "slay the Dragon" for the betterment of the whole, you find your family of people that look after each other but not covering for bad ideas, yet helping to make a misguided idea, that in theory has merit, but requires the other talents of all to fine tune and implement the new idea.

The best part is when they treat you as an equal, but allows you to be "One of Them", yet respecting the rank and title you hold, while you respect their contribution and efforts. The absolute joy of working in this environment is without measure. It stops becoming work and becomes a livelihood, manifesting a army without limits to the proportion of their talent or contributions to all aspects of the company, without jealous, back-biting, and office politics reduces itself to a bare minimum. The employee that sells you, may be doing so out of pure excitement, but may be working you over instead, to see or find the boundaries; his limits, as he or she may not may not believe in his idea but may be seeing if you will buy them in an attempt to judge your depth of intelligence. This employee needs to have the opportunity to reap the defeat or success of the idea alone, not involving other, so the failure will be all theirs, without others to hide behind or throw rocks or arrows of accusations, but to embrace and commit their ideas solely to their brain and the worth of the company. A close watch must be kept on this one, as to catch them before they waste to much of the companies resources, or allowing them to use title that others will become ineffective in trying to help them manifest a poor ineffective idea.

The lists of personalities are a three circus of wonderful spontaneous pro-actiove warriors as you unleash them to think, act, react, respond, produce, and make the company a mirror image of them.

For you CEOs and Presidents, be the switchboard operator for a day, or better yet, mop the lobby floor or clean the bathroom using your work ethic to produce an outstanding result and sit back and watch you title take on an amazing new power. But do these jobs, regardless what they are, with absolute respect asking others how you can do your job better. This is leading by example, not talking about it.

Remember that you, and you alone, create the work environment; Good or bad! It is who you are; "who yo' mama and daddy raised". Actually it is who God himself created you to be.

Chapter Five

"Can I walk across your back, so I can feel a little taller?"

I can remember once my little boy, Daniel, asked me, "What do you do at Daddy?" I thought only for a brief, sobering moment and answered him in a way that was a little much for a small child to understand, however, as a Father, I told him the truth.

Yet this time I questioned the depth of my thoughts, as he only wanted to know if I was a fireman, a policeman or a Doctor; I think, at times, as a parent I have actually become all three. Maybe I had really become a great fireman since I had become such a great arsonist, creating my own problems and having to solve them myself. I soulfully replied to my son,

"Son, I work amongst thieves...I work amongst thieves...those that would steal the simple joys from those yearning to have a livelihood, instead of a job, and worse yet, those that attempt to secretly steal, or dilute, the fortunes of child's inheritance, given by birthright, from a King...ask me not to talk, touch, nor pick up the weapons of

a cowardly thief, for I cannot, nor will not. Instead, I choose to focus on the strengths and silent determination of the openly brave...the workers, for Son, I work amongst thieves. Yet...Take heart, for Hope will prevail, Empowerment is at hand, and there is much work to do".

I have found this truth all of my life as I have delved into the many companies that have been assigned me, or that I have won, rightly, or wrongly on the "Field of Battle". Needless to say the sadness of human nature brings me to my knees to pray for my enemies, only to find that the enemies are my very comrades assigned to me, locked away in fear, and in a jealous rage. A rage that the lost and downtrodden feed within themselves, that they might never be given the hope to arise. It would even seem that some seek failure for their co-workers. If a worker attempts to rise above normalcy, their co-workers fear they, themselves, will be seen as weak, in comparison, or not as important, in a direct comparison to the co-worker that is attempting to rise to a place of personal excellence. This is such a sad indictment of human nature and of the human race. Yet this condition is real and happens everyday, regularly and usually within arms length of our desk. Just watch as someone tries to dig out of a trench and see how many people are waiting in line to kick them back down.

To lead the legions of the lost, begging for the blind hope of victory, not ever really understanding, nor being able to calculate the weight of the battle, yet having the courage to rise up, to be pitted against the faceless drones called co-workers, manipulated by fear, seen daily in common sight, who suffer a dead, painful life, dedicated to a purpose of insuring their own sick and self serving comfort. Using methods in which tears down anyone that attempts to rise above normalcy, or ascend to a level of hope, or of personal contribution, or personal excellence.

Could it be the fear or a demonic disease that is passed from generation to generation, gene to gene, predestined from the womb to tear away at the possibilities of another's life, by making it ok to be like everyone else, to be content to preach, through paranoia, in some purposeful prose, that yields some sick joy, that makes it perfectly normal to be like everyone else, regardless of their behavior, their beliefs, their spin on what success is, or what makes a person fulfilled and worthy.

Regardless from whatever foxhole, pit, ditch or bland, purpose-less life you might awaken from, or to, there is always the freedom of hope; yet only for those who are not intimidated by their fear.

A very good friend of mine, Dr. Frank Hyles a Methodist minister, once said, "Courage is not the absence of fear, but is doing what is right in the face of fear". Dr. Hyles is right on the money. He usually was; his Boss made sure of that. Frank listened a lot to his Boss. Frank's boss empowered him.

It continues to amaze me that empowerment fosters alibis that explain, or attempts to explain away failure, or even validate pure laziness in an individual. I can think of the countless reasons which I have heard why someone can't do a particular thing, reciting the rhetoric of lost hope or misplaced trust. It is my life's experience and absolute belief, as well as my first hand knowledge that all is possible and even probable, if one tries. You know the saying, "We can do anything. The impossible just takes a little longer".

The commitment to ones self to rise above the norm, or to rise above the one sitting next to you at work that is happy with normalcy, for whatever reason, cannot and must not flavor your vision, or the description, or understanding of your own life, or its potential for achievements.

One must be very strong in their beliefs if one is going to conquer the demons of "can't". You have got to be pretty strong to endure the snide comments made behind your back, or pretty thick skinned to face those brave enough to voice their distaste, for your efforts to succeed and to overcome, directly to your face.

Love yourself before trying to show love to another. Listen to your own sermons before expecting others to listen to them. Walk the walk, talk the talk, but be an example to yourself. I heard it once said somewhere, by somebody sometime, "Am I the man, that I as a child, would want to call Daddy". A sobering, humbling thought considering my Dad died when I was only eight. My dad was John Wayne, Roy Rogers and Superman all rolled up into one; a hard act for me to follow as I attempt to be a "Dad", at work and at home.

Chapter Six

When Armor becomes an Anchor

As a salesman since birth, at least it seems so, I have learned that overcoming objections, or facing the word "no" takes a layer or two, off your hide, off of your very self-worth, off your own opinion of yourself. To face the word "no" day after day, hoping, working, planning, and struggling to hear the single most important word in your vocabulary, the word "yes", is a search that tears away at the very fiber in which you consider yourself made from, and of.

As a salesman or a leader, we adorn ourselves with armor known to salesmen as confidence, although some call it, or have called it arrogance, not knowing the difference between the two. As the salesman wears his confidence bravely, such as a warrior would wear his battle armor, the warrior's armor takes blow after blow, hit after hit, the same as hearing the word "no" time and time again. A salesman, as a warrior must pick himself up, dust himself off, re-bend his armor, sharpen his sword and begin his battle, again.

As a warrior, or salesman, when given the task of leadership, or worse yet executive management, he faces the same demons as that of the salesmen, yet now it is his own troops that silently say "no". As is the case more often than not, the silence of "no" from an employee, is a deliberate act of defiance, an absolute and deliberate resentment of authority placed above them, yielding the same feeling as when the customer screams "no" by saying, "yes, thank you, have a nice day, I will be sending in my order", yet never does.

The employee can be the same as the client that never lets you in to see him or know him. They can also be like the customer that does let you in to see him, mostly out of courtesy, but is the one that does not respond to a word that you say, nor reacts or acts to anything proclaimed within your presentation of product, or service, or, as for an employee, listens to your direct orders, or agrees with everything you say, but implements nothing.

Now, as the salesman, turned manager, leader, or executive supervisor, facing the art of selling the mission or the strategy, to his own troops, now attempts to do what he has done so many times before, although when he finds himself face down in the dirt, alone in his failure and fear; he quickly, in desperation, reverts to old weapons, or techniques, old strategies that once yielded success on the field of battle. He re-enforces his armor with confidence to sustain the last attempted mortal wound, or the inter-company arrow in the back.

As he applies layer after layer to his armor, the armor gets heavier and heavier, becoming a debilitating weight that turns itself into the anchor and his confidence can turn itself into pure and ugly arrogance. At that point, the once valiant warrior, glorious on the field of battle through his resolve and determination fails, for his armor is too heavy and he cannot rise. He cannot even stand up. The warrior's armor has now grounded the champion, as the weight of carrying the arrogance of self has turned him into a defeated, arrogant, self-important waste of time and breath.

When failure, and the inability to affect change are realized, the panic the warrior experiences are so great that neither weapon nor the armor that once served the warrior works. The armor becomes a disgusting, impotent tool of battle, clothing of doom and of self-destruction. Worse yet, the warrior that lies on the ground defeated believes that he has won, by and through the thickness of his armor, or self-importance. Yet the battle passes above him, without allowing him entry into the fight. He lies there defeated, unable to fight, or even acknowledge that the battle rages around him. Only through self-analysis, does a true warrior know the strength of his armor's metal. He also knows when to wear it and when not to.

On the field of battle, as in executive management, many brave and noble field warriors, or salesman, deserve the fruits of past battles, the spoils of war and title, yet they cannot articulate the change from warrior to general. The modern spoil of war is the "Promotion", the recognition; Whether it is from warrior to general to king, or from salesmen to executive manager or CEO. A great warrior may very likely make a great General, in that the General most likely has the experience as the ultimate warrior. Yet he may not possess the ability of wisdom, or the knowledge of leadership, or techniques of empowerment to become King.

The battle, the war, or the struggle, whether it is today, yesterday or a thousand years from now, I beseech you, to think of the General, for he too is scared, he too questions his right and his appointment to lead; questioning his qualifications, his call to service. He that questions himself is worthy to follow; yet, he is only worthy to follow due to his humility, due to his heart, due to his passion, and his deep appreciation for, and of those that blindly and boldly follow him into the battle, the battle of self; a brutal battle of self that is beyond earthly purportion.

(Excepts from the writings **"The General and his Fear"** by Rod Richardson)

"I stand adorned in the golden armor of a God I have never known, but yet longingly attempt to, through my pitiful cravings and callings, called to service, from a humble and dirt poor beginning, to stand before the brave hearts of thousands, masses of the hopeful, trusting warriors, anticipating the horrors, and the heroes, of the battle before them. I, as their General, stand

proud, but painfully confused, at how, or why, I have been called to lead.

A General, I am, a leader of leaders, a commander of brave hearts that will gladly die and take their last breath speaking, even screaming my name, not in dismay, but in the glory to serve.

What immeasurable weight! It is almost unbearable; I don't believe I can hold such weight on these trembling and terrified legs of this so-called General. I must command, I must be strong, if not for me, but for them; the trusting, the followers of a single spirit – mine, and mission before us – a being from humble roots, elevated, not by choice, but by a predestined appointment to a place that I so truly fear. Will I be strong enough, brave enough, to face their faces, as they die in battle, and yet face my own death as well, with the regrets and the confusion, of why I was called to service?

What did I have of such importance to yield such a noble appointment? What did the Gods see in this humble frame, that I do not, nor do I understand? What piece, or part of me, makes me worthy to lead such brave, honest and loyal men onto the field of battle? To face the hordes of horror before me is not the enemy, but my enemy is the doubt I have in my own ability, an invisible ability seen by others, but cruelly invisible to me.

I stand assured, sharpened sword in hand, awaiting the charge of the impending enemy, to feel the full weight of fear within my mind, to come nose to nose with the enemy, the real enemy - my own fear, inside this trembling and terrified heart.

There is a moment that you see and feel fear, come face to face with it, and in a millisecond, a wisp of time, you raise your sword high, facing impending doom, and you swing your cold and calculated blade with the courage and the viciousness of the evil that stands before you. Without regard for your safety, but with complete commitment to destroy, and gleefully watch your fear, lie split into, bleeding its' blood of doom onto your feet, as you run the blade of your sword, over and over again through the throat of the enemy, as to say, "I will prevail, I will survive, I will empower others, I will slay the evil that disempowers mankind".

Battles, regardless of size, yield the same results. Legions of the hopeful, the brave, and the cowards killed by their own troops, the internal fear of real leaders, or the fear within generals in this case, the enemy is always the same – FEAR; The fear that we will fail, that we will die without purpose, or meaning.

To embrace and successfully carry out the charge of leadership, particularly the leadership of warriors, or any talented God-given being that serves under your leadership or command, you, as the leader, must understand the word, "servant".

The armor must be removed. A leader must become familiar standing bare and vulnerable, trusting those beneath him to fight the twins of terror, fear and self. Evangelist, Joyce Meyers explains fear as an acronym, "False Evidence Appearing Real". I think she is dead on the money.

Empowering leaders need their energy to lead. Fear fosters worry and worry is an exhausting, debilitating disease. Positive actions, encouragement and articulated plans are this disease's cure. The manager must attempt to impart his visions to those beneath them, while working to release the talents and visions within each, one to another.

Excepts from "the General and his Fear" – Rod Richardson

"An armor with a King's crest,

that he so bravely wore,

that had taken

such a relentless

and savage beating

from the enemies of the throne,

from within his own beloved Kingdom,

from traitors

within his own ranks,

his brothers in arms,

that would kill their own,

all for a chance for glory,

although

a dishonest glory,

His armor had survived betrayal,

As well as honest enemy attack,

this tired and noble armor

worn by this proud man,

once broken to pride,

by his God,

to now embrace the name of servant,

instead of that of Lord and Master;

his armor had held strong.

his eyes still brutally defiant,

even though the battle was,

for the most part over.

His battered, bloodied frame,

his tired eyes of steel blue strength,

his relentless,

once terrified heart,

had arisen to prevail,

persecute,

destroy

and to conquer

the Kingdom's enemy,

the hordes of the dishonest,

from inside and out,

the evil thieves,

all enemies

using the weapons of disempowerment,

as well as facing

the decisive and deliberate destruction

of his own internal fear,

while enduring

the epic and enormous

horrors,

of a cruel

and deliberate war".

The armor of the warrior, or the leader, must be respected yet must be taken off as the warrior places himself in a general's or an executive leadership role. The only true and pure protective armor that a leader can wear is that of the very people that they lead. To his subordinates, to be strong, is to wear a coat of armor that is invisible yet invincible, through the collective talents of all that follow this empowering leader.

To lead such an army is to lead a force of power beyond earthly explanation. It is to truly become a "Servant King" by the ultimate empowerment of others. To ask the questions, "What can I do to help you today"?, "What can I do to help you accomplish the goals I have given you"?, "What can I do to help you today?"

Leaders, I dare you...try it and see where it leads. If you have created an environment that yields you receiving honest answers from your troops, you will be amazed at where it will lead. I dare you, ask the question. Strip away the rank and title and become a real team of one mind. Never disrespecting the service of those that give it, nor allowing anyone to disrespect a title of rank, which was given through what has been earned. As a boss, just because you have the bat, does not mean you have to use it. Use something different...your brain.

Chapter Seven

Power without Pride

The violence, the rough and physically hurtful stuff like you might see on TV, rarely happens unless you work for the type of men and women that built, bought or stole companies, and the dreams of others in that manner.

In this environment, the terror and abuse becomes somewhat normal and horribly, just another day at the office. We must get past the reality of that side of business that unfortunately exists – it is criminal. To these types of warriors in this environment, the word "business" is just a justifiable excuse for the brutality that lives within them by their own demonic nature. In reality, the deeds and actions of these abusive and, perceived, powerful managers, are generally based upon their own fear; the fear of losing this painful and pathetic power. It is not the loss of money, or the loss of earthly possessions, but the loss of manipulating, or conforming people through their acts of abuse and intimidation.

We have all had some examples of these methods right before our eyes, if nothing else on TV, which, more often that not, emulates reality. The way to overcome this paralysis of a company inflected upon you is to call it what it is; arrogance and ego. This sick leadership approach destroys the good deeds and methods that are found and employed daily, by our subordinates, which will overcome this disease by addressing the symptoms directly, face to face, person to person.

The symptoms of this disease are caused by the installation of a perverse, defeating and destructive power of one's power over another. The cure is to virtually face-off the fear and intimidation, confront it, the lies and the surrendering spin, which has been installed upon you by your enemies, or worse installed upon yourself, by yourself. The immediate rejection of the opposing power, by utilizing the same assertion of power that is used upon you, without the degradation of your own character, or the character of others, is at your very command. To recognize your power to replace fear with hope is the tool for the decisive death of such an opposing power.

Your enemy's installation of fear upon you, or the employment of your enemy's creation of perceived fact, or the tearing down of your self-worth, renders you as powerless, without mind or worth. It will make you a sudden slave to this degradation and its evil delivering you to your enemy. Your very reactions are not of your own desires, thoughts or natural will, but in fact, it is a cunning weapon, used by your enemy to control your actions and strategies.

It is at this very moment that the realization of your enemy's power over you becomes real. You experience the feeling, the coldness and emptiness of fear. It is when you embrace this fear as a fact of the lack of your self worth, that this tactic of war devours you. In this moment of absolute panic and fear, you are ultimately defined as a leader as you choose to act or react, based upon your enemies personal will and agendas placed upon and within you, and what you enemy has decided that you will be – defeated and powerless.

There are plenty of poor souls that know the real world of war, but choose to pretend, or to play within it, within their own controlled environments in which they humanly create. They pretend to be a leader, a warrior, in a place where they always win, where they play childish games, ironically called mind, or power games all the while afraid to go out into the real world of war, where death and failure will gladly greet them.

Destined by their actions and inactions, never to gain, or find themselves through true inter-growth, the worth of their company, or of themselves; never finding the actual rewards that accompany their God-given gifts by seeking out, and understanding the characteristics of the real battle. They never actually walk out onto the field of battle. They never passionately wage a war on normalcy and lost hope, nor do they invite the destruction of the demons that controls their dead, desolate and deserted mind; never meeting themselves as warriors.

It is not the battle that is brutal it is the fear that keeps you from the fight that is so horribly savage. It strips a person of their self-esteem; yet creates a self-inflating pride. It makes good-minded people, mean-spirited; it makes a person, unjustly, take out their own personal rage, their disappointments, fears, and anger on others, and in some cases, the very people that follow them into battle. It destroys the very souls that count on their leader's productive and positive actions for their very living. (i.e. house payment)

It causes a pretentious leader to seek out the weak as their field captains, as their confidants, counselors, all in the name of leadership, yielding control; a cheap imitation of power, a self-serving demon of destruction called pride, arrogance or ego.

The real power that eludes them and the power, of which I speak of, is the power to BE YOURSELF, as God made you. To stand confident whichever direction the wind may blow, and whichever enemy, or demon, stands before you, internal or external. This power deserves the respect of all that choose to follow and abide by it; it is a power to cross any bridge, to embrace any positive change, at any time. It is the ability to articulate the goodness and joy inside of you, directly in the face of evil, without using like evil to combat the demons, which seek to destroy you, or seeks to dilute your ability to lead others to their own personal, and/or collective victory.

Using force against like-force, using deliberate tools of war instantly, without hesitation in order to destroy fear, quickly and decisively, within yourself, and within all that follow you is to know pure and positive power. Again your powers are, again, those beneath you that you lead and their contributions to the battle at hand.

In this war, there have been very few times that men are destroyed by the enemies outside the kingdom walls. They are destroyed by the fear that resides within them, or the fear they have manufactured within their own walls. This is the weapon that yields the most destruction to the leader's soul and spirit; Walls that serve as our own personal prison, shackled by our own installed fears; fears that paralyze the hopes and the promise of our daily deeds, desires and struggles.

Learning how to utilize, implement and execute this fear, toward and within your enemy is the single most used, destructive as well as productive weapons, in corporate America. It makes your enemy, or opponent lose focus on the real battle and makes them concentrate of things that will, more likely than not, never happen. It makes them doubt self. It is a disease that knows not the difference between arrogance and self-confidence. It is a kind of a selective, installed, personal paranoia placed within you by your enemy. It is your enemy making you the enemy to yourself.

If you don't know and cannot recognize this threat or fear, or recognize it as real, or cannot recognize the things which your enemy has deliberately installed upon you and which ones weren't, you will never know how to respond and/or defeat this demon; helpless to fight, when it stands right before you, or within you.

This threat, or fear, is only as big, and mighty as you make it. It derives its life and size from what importance you give it, from perceptions you create within your own mind; fed and cared for by your own hand, at the expense of your own self-esteem and self worth.

You have power, an awesome undeniable, unstoppable power of leadership, a power placed within you from birth, installed by God. You have always had it. However, the deliberate recognition, and the purposeful employment of this power, without the destructive and self-centered nature of pride will always be the hardest part in the use of this power, as well as having the potential to be your enemy's greatest weapon.

As for why you fight? You have a purpose! A meaning! A life! Let no one steal it from you, or the joy it possesses, regardless of who they are that seeks it, or the size or the importance of what they want it for, or they demand of its use. You can, and you must stand in the face of fear and not flinch, nor even acknowledge it as a power. Neither fear, nor your enemies control you, only you control you. Seek the grace of God and the fruits of the gifts God have granted you as a leader.

"The difficulty of this challenge is not to allow power to turn into pride. For pride is cheap armor. It can never stop the blade of truth, nor can it withstand the heat of the humble.

Within each kingdom, or company, there are many brave souls, as well as many, that are lost to hope, too scared to seek it, too weak to fight for it or too proud to pray for it. For there are many that seek to take you to the depths of their daily defeat, as they themselves, decidedly, descend daily to their dungeon of doom. Thereby, you, as they, are constantly being diluted or worse yet, destroyed, by going with them on their path, unconscious to what is happening in an effort for them to feel normal at your expense.

Be whom God has created, nothing more, nothing less, but flawless unto Gods' perfect will for you and your ultimate service and contributions to yourself and to your fellow man.

To Be, or Not To Be…that was never the question. "Be" what God has created. Remember that God does not make Junk. He is in the business of making "jewels from junk".

Chapter Eight

The Recipe

We that have been given much, much is expected! I challenge you to examine the following in your own company, even within your own life. Define and explore the following:

1. **Our Strategy as it relates to the individual battles, as well as the overall war.**

2. **Our clear understanding of the opposing enemy, external and internal.**

3. **Our utilization of our resources: human, technological, financial and physical.**

4. **Our organizational structure, as it is directly matched to the strategy selected.**

5. Internal empires and personalities that defeat from within.

6. Our ability to listen, and hear between the words.

7. To think beyond the boundaries of our own intelligence

8. To achieve an environment that endorses it's **OK** to say, "I don't know, but, as a **TEAM**, we'll find out".

9. To execute, based not on where we have been, but where we **"CHOOSE"** to go.

10. Retain and protect our single greatest asset, each other, our personal self worth and the value of our brand's equity.

Let's talk about these ten little jewels for a while.

To examine each of these requires not only self-examination but also the analytical value of the mission, the war, the tools or requirements of battle, and most importantly the harmony, one to another, to obtain a successful and organized victory. These are not the ten commandments of the "New Testament of Business Leadership", but they are close. Those must be interpreted from your own self-analysis and make your own recipe from scratch. This recipe, if followed, that will lead to the analysis of mission, of self, of supplies, knowledge of your troops and of the overall scope of the war that you intend to wage.

In battle we fight, plan and work hard, to win territory for our Kingdom. In today's world, we put on armor, most of the times called a "suit", pick up our sword, now called a "presentation" and fight for the land and bounty of another kingdom and for the recognition of our superior power, all in the name of market share and/or brand equity.

To breakdown this battle plan for analysis, and not in any particular order, the following ten topics address many of the gut wrenching conditions that dis-empowers talented employees and causes leaders to wonder, "why they lost the war", or causes an employee to seek another job, worse yet, losing the livelihood they have worked for and that they have, historically, enjoyed.

1. The Strategy as it relates to the individual battles, as well as the overall war.

"What are we doing?"; Why did we do that?; Whose bright idea was this anyway?; Don't they know how bad this will hurt my department?; I can't believe we pay people like this; Where did they go to school? Did they even go to school? Where is he from?, Where did they get her? This is embarrassing", "I have a reputation to think about".

All these questions, and many more, are directly related to trying to sing the hymn, but not being on the same page of the hymnal. They tend to accuse, blame, belittle, and betray; each one of them the battle cry of the lost and the defeated.

When a company engages, or embarks upon a strategy, that is usually done in the form of a marketing plan, or a business plan sometimes it is as simple as a company's "Mission Statement", more likely than not it is page after page of research, action plans, and reactions, with as keen eye on the product, the competition and the customer.

Often employees don't respond to the strategy, nor to the battle, but tend to pay more attention to a shortsighted, self-centered manager, or inter-company political influences, as they approach common, daily problems and individual job responsibilities. Not really knowing why they do what they do, or actually having, or being allowed, through a forced environment of fear, to voice a better way of doing things.

Instead, a non-visionary manager, or fellow-employee cuts them short of a solutions implementation or even a solid suggestion.

Mostly change is derailed through apathy, by those with a lack of self-confidence, or an individual's opinion of the idea's importance, generally based on a feeling that no one will listen to them anyway. However the bedrock of this apathy is fear.

When we hire people it should be for how, and who they are, and for all of what they are, including all of their life's experiences freely exposing and utilizing their god-given talents toward the strategy laid before them and the company. Employees, or managers should require talents that have nothing to do with where they went to school, or their popularity, or of their political standing within the company.

The strategy of a company has to be clearly defined and communicated to all of the employees right down to the guy that cuts the grass, or washes the windows, right up to the CEO, or President of the company, or whomever the people are that are actually defining the plan and putting in place the plan's tactics and the plan's people utilization. It is not good enough to write a job description without discussing how it will be integrated into the overall strategy of the company, and how it will be realized and utilized to win the war.

As the plan's tactics are calculated, it must flow directly to each and every job, and to each and every person that is under the leaders command. A leader must evaluate the importance of the job or the worth of the person holding it. A leader must continually ask himself, or herself the ultimately question: Is there a need for the person, a need for the job, and how do they both fit within the company's operating organization and confirm the fact that they are not wasting financial resources by allowing the job's mere existence.

If everyone is singing in the company choir understands how the tune goes, they are more able to sing the song, in the same key, at the same time, and hence sound like a choir, making music; instead of an undesirable and deafening noise of failure with no purpose or plan. The harmony between employee, job, department, division, corporation, whatever the structure is, top to bottom, is an absolute key to carrying the strategy to an effective, efficient end.

A leader ignoring in-fighting and not realizing, or acting upon its cause, unleashes the catastrophic effect these internal battles can have on a corporations overall strategy and dooms the plan to fail before even beginning the war. Attention must paid constantly, right down to the abuse of an employee having the wrong job, suffering and living a miserable work life, due to your election of the person in a particular position is of supreme importance. This employee's home life probably isn't much better. I really bet that person would be a joy at home after suffering the misuse and abuse of being in the wrong job and suffering through it day after day. (Pardon the sarcasm)

A healthy exchanges of ideas, or the exchange of opposing viewpoints are one thing; but the key evaluating element of appraising this activity, as positive or negative, is the level of respect employed as this occurs, based both upon the individual employee as a person and the rank and file conditions that exist. Watch and listen carefully. This takes practice and lots of it. Watch, look, and listen carefully. Don't jump to appearances.

2. The clear understanding of the opposing enemy, external and internal.

Having a clear and full understanding of the enemy is absolutely imperative to the successful outcome of the war you wage. Not understanding this within the very war you have pledged to fight, your victory will be seriously jeopardized, and as with it, the cause of the mission of your organization and the very purpose for the organization under your immediate direction and command. Who is the enemy?

The external enemy is easy. It's the other guy. It is the enemy that has your customer's business or the competitor that has the market share your company needs or expects to capture.

A clear knowledge of the enemy's strength, and their propensity for their actions, beyond your assumed predications, is without equal in preparing your battle plan or your strategy of attack.

Never, I again repeat, never, assume their actions in war based upon what you would do, because, you are not them and they are not you. Prepare your battle plans and strategies based on what "they" have done before or could do based strictly upon the fact, of "they" being they, not on assumptions of what you would do if you traded places with the enemy. Do the homework. Study the opponent.

This requirement requires study, learning, observations of the enemy's past actions, and knowing that we all tend to lean on, or go back to, what is comfortable, or what is familiar. Placing yourself in their mind, based on who they are. That is the secret of knowing your enemy, not based on your own intellect, but based upon what your opponent has demonstrated, within their actions, their actual historical deeds demonstrated.

Although placing your energies on knowing the external enemy can be tough, the internal enemy is tougher. By now you are starting to get the picture on the internal enemy. The internal enemy is us. It is the demons we feed, by our own hands, daily, that rob us of our personal growth, accomplishments and the ability to reach for excellence through the fulfillment of ourselves by the use of our natural talents and through the encouragement and empowerment of others.

3. The utilization of our resources: human, technological, financial and physical.

All four resources, human, technological, financial, and physical are equally important. To believe that one is more important than the other is absurd. It reminds me of departments within a company that fight for the spotlight of glory, as they compete for who is more important, as compared to the other.

I can remember one time at a sales conference a vice-president of sales telling a controller, "that the sales department makes the history, controllers just record it".

We all want to be special. We all want to be important in the eyes of our peers and in the eyes of our subordinates. Yet we tend to do it on the backs of those around us and not solely on the merits of our work. "Let me walk upon your back so I can feel a little taller".

As I have said, I feel the greatest tragedy that corporate America faces today is the mis-utilization of its human resources, it inability to really listen, and the mis-utilization of our co-workers and managers. The quicker we come to the realization that as a team our success is completely based on those around us, on how human interactions are employed, and on how solutions transpire, the quicker we get to the real subject matter - **"SOLUTIONS ARE GROWN FROM THE**

BOTTOM UP, DIRECTIVES ARE NOT DRIVEN DOWN FROM THE TOP".

The technological, financial, and physical elements of the company, or team are equally important. None are more important than the other.

The application of arrogance of one's importance over another dilutes the combined power of all of the vital resources. Logically, to place technological advancement of research over the financial ability to complete a project, to win a battle for brand equity, is the same as having a low-cost, efficient bottled water plant in the middle of the desert. The term comes to mind, "all dressed up and nowhere to go".

"Got everything we need to make a profit, now all we need to do is find some water". An unbalanced company that focuses on operations, or finance, instead of sales, could have said this; for a little while at least.

Again, all aspects of the resources afforded a company, or a cause must be balanced, one to another, and in the proportional use of each; measured, protected and employed. The very same scenarios exist within understanding the importance of each other and the importance of each individual department, singularly and/or combined.

In a successful company all of these resources are equally important to the successful outcome of a battle, or the desired outcome of the entire war. It is the leader, similar to a conductor of an orchestra, that knows when to call for, and when and how to, employee the human resources to make profitable music.

Separate the four areas mentioned above, study them individually and related one to another. If they are not working within an environment that flatter and glorify each other, the leader has some work to do, and the leaders under him or her.

4. The organizational structure, as it is directly matched to the strategy selected.

The organization, as an organism, a living form, is like the corporate structure as a whole. It has a life, a purpose, and a reason for an existence. Its purpose is to provide the foundation for all the inter-actions between the workers, employees, customers, suppliers that attempt to flourish and live within it and around it, and make a profit, or a paycheck in the process.

Most corporations use organizational charts showing rank and file scenarios for the separation between classes of workers, or responsibilities, as in "executive management" or "just employees", as if the word "just" is even relevant when discussing, or addressing any employee.

The integrity of the corporate organization, as well as the positions within them, must be accommodated with a level of respect for the position, or the title, not necessarily the person that holds it, although it does help. **Remember respect is earned, not granted.**

The organizational structure must be matched in fit, form, and function to the battle and strategy at hand. It must meet the recognized needs and demands for action in the field of battle, as well as the actions behind the line of fire back at headquarters. To attempt to do battle, without having respect for the titles of the organization chart that one works within, is to disrespect the function of the department, the corporation, and undermines the strategic control of each part of the entire company as it attempts to work together within a common goal.

Just because you do not like someone does not give you the right to ignore, or disrespect the function of the title and its need thereof. To omit someone, in writing, or in some significant company action from others that are involved in carrying out specific strategic parts of a plan, solely due to one's personality or one's difference in opinions, is to disrespect the title's importance and worth and the ultimate need for the department, and its contribution as a whole.

The corporate structure, and the strategies the corporation undertakes, must be guarded and maintained regardless and must remain consistent in content and form, aligned with the strategies and goals that lie before it.

All organizations require constant change and must constantly implement new strategies in order to stay alive and remain prosperous and effective in the market. If the corporate structure changes every time the company faces a specialized, departmental problem, they erase the integrity of the entire corporate structure as a whole.

The same holds true if the person who effects the change is based on jealousy, or feels threatened by the actions, or opinions of an opposing person, instead of looking for the value of their opinion based on their intelligence, or their God-given gifts and talents that you may not possess. One that ignores or intentionally excludes a key member of the corporate staff, to be part of a team, to a carry out a mission, or seeks solutions to solve a particular problem, solely based on the likes, or dislikes, of the person, or a person's inability to embrace an idea that is not of their thinking, routinely and effectively destroys the entire integrity of the complete and whole corporate structure.

These laser-guided missiles shot from laser-guided, non-guns destroys the worth of the corporate executives function and more than likely the entire department. Respect must be given to the title and the titles' function within the corporate structure, however, one does not have to like or agree with the person filling the position or carrying the title. But one must allow for everyone to be involved and participate in all the endeavors of the mission, if nothing more than providing knowledge of ones' own actions, or that of a department.

As for a CEO, President, or General, one must ask why they are not confronting the problem with an individual's personality, instead hiding behind the act of reorganization to solve the problem. Removing the person entirely from the company might remove problems reaching far down the line of command when an empowering leader that teaches empowerment, as well as practices what they preach, replaces the person removed. Unless of course if the person is the President of other absolute top-executive If this sniper attack upon the integrity of the corporation is due to someone not wanting confrontation with the person, or the problem, perhaps someone should shoot the General, or CEO.

Frankly, if a leader dilutes the title of his department, or another, by allowing a reorganization of the corporate entity due to individuals inability to work beyond their personal feelings or has a over sensitivity to another departments failures, the corporate structure will never have the integrity of function, nor will it have durability within it's rank and file, and ultimately it's order. A corporation or department will not possess the resolve, or the character, nor can it withstand the rigors of battle, much less the war.

The leader, or department head, must go beyond the measurements of people based on worldly, self-centered standards and ultimately look beyond company politics and popularity when assigning the proper personnel and title, as the person, the job and the title are fitted for the war and for it's strategy.

The object of fine tuning the corporate structure from the top down requires a selfless leader that expects selfless acts of leadership by all those that they promote, or empower, and by the encouragement and empowerment of all those that work beneath them.

The leader must rise above the bland standards of mediocrity and find their own personal self-excellence through helping all beneath them find their place within the strategy, within the mission, within the company and in all that is to be undertaken.

5. The Internal empires and personalities that defeat from within.

Not having everyone dialed in, or tuned in to the strategy selected for the successful outcome of the mission writes the epitaph for the funeral of your mission, and possibly your company, long before its death on the field of battle.

Not being tuned in to all the diseases and demons inside an organization is just as fatal, if not more so. To list a few: jealousy, low-self-esteem, lack of confidence, being someone you are not, fear of honesty in your opinions, greed, multiple individual kingdoms within the same kingdom, ego, procrastination, lack of positive or empowering attitudes, self-glorification or arrogance, a lack of general positive, solution seeking attitudes, keeping score on another, lack of morals, fear of failure, basic fear in general, bringing problems at home to work, lack of empathy, individual non-business personal problems, drug or alcohol dependency, internal sexual romances between co-workers, failure to make individual self-analysis, failure to fully embrace strengths and weaknesses and above all, not embracing the strategy as a whole, or tilting the outcome of missions to serve only yourself and your ego. Still want to be a leader? You got be kidding?

To address all of these, would be is to write another book. I am sure each of us could., or at least a lengthy article. Each has an individual set of requirements for the leader to deal with and to implement solutions through honest and direct communications addressing each through honest, fearless, evaluation and employing the knowledge to fix the ones you can, and to acknowledge, and accept the ones that you can't, while knowing the difference between the two.

A leader must be aware of the task before him or her and the things that will cause them to stumble. "God grant me the wisdom to know what I can change, and what I can't, and the difference between the two".

6. The ability to listen, and hear between the words.

The key to this impossibility is to learn to "listen louder". Sounds impossible. The frustration would be equal to an untrained teacher trying to teach an ADD child. A similarity in attempting to teach or deal with the child's ADD symptoms, such as dyslexia, using methods and commands of scolding the child to look a word harder, when the child actually has another step in the learning process of turning the word around, backwards in their mind, before the child can attempt to read it. It is impossible to look at something harder, or to listen to something louder. This idea or tactic becomes a cruel and demeaning drill because you cannot look at something any harder than looking at it, or casting your sight upon it. If you see it, you see it; there is nothing more you can do. If you hear it you hear it, if you don't, the same applies.

Yet trying to figure out the motives behind the interactions with subordinates, one to another, can turn you into Sherlock Holmes, or, at the very least, a person that is not much fun to be around. If all you ever do is analyze every singe thing said to you or around you, pretty soon it will be very quite wherever you go. In this case, you will spend more time trying to figure out what somebody is trying to tell you, diluting your power as a leader, than just accepting what is actually being told, and moving on. However, when dialing in the strategy, and discussing new possibilities and new ideas, whether it is new aspects of a person's current job, or reorganizing a current organization, mission, or strategy, it is imperative to listen as loud as you possibly can, even between the words not said.

You may not be hearing honest valid points, as the strategy is being dissected and appraised, but instead you may be hearing fear of change, one of the multiple diseases I mentioned earlier. Recognizing the characteristic of a co-workers low self-esteem as motives of their responses are made visible to the leader that listens, but only to the leaders that listen, as much or more than they talk.

There are spaces between the words you hear; the things not said. The things not made audible through the spoken word. You must remember the power of words. It was words, powerful words, such as that of God's words, as reported in the book of Genesis, which when spoken by God, created the entire heaven and earth. The things that are not said are very powerful and very descriptive of the possibilities and /or opinions that exist and that are available for use.

A spoken answer to a question is defined as an answer, but not giving an answer to a question that is directly asked, is also an answer. This unemotional action of a non-answer must be addressed and calculated as a direct plan of your opposition's strategy. All aspects of your intellect must be used and alert in order that you might understand the question, decision or direction being asked of you. Sometimes a person informing you of something is not reporting or advising, but actually asking for your permission or acceptance of an action yet to be taken.

7. To think beyond the boundaries of our own intelligence

Get out of the box; think beyond the boundaries of your own intelligence. Sounds impossible but it is not to the empowering leader. Power exists when one is not threatened by the work, thoughts, or the intelligence of others, or refuses to buy into the self-defeating attributes of someone having low self-worth or low-self self-esteem.

Just as arrogance can tear apart the good intentions of a leader, similarly a poor opinion of the ideas, intelligence and solutions of the very people that follow you, steals not only your credibility as a leader, but denies you the benefits of the gifts of others; gifts and intellect that you do not possess but may employ through those that are in your command.

President Ronald Reagan was labeled as the great communicator, however, his greatest asset as a leader, was to run interference for the great people which he employed to follow him, and to carry out his missions and strategies. He surrounded himself with tons of talent; People that were truly gifted in ways that Reagan didn't have a clue of how to think, or proceed, with the next step of the plan required. Reagan led by following, and recognizing the gifts and intelligence of others. He did not rely on his own skills that of being a great actor but relied on the intelligence of those he hired to make him the ultimate leader.

Placing people in charge of areas that Reagan did not understand and empowering them to succeed within their individual goals was his talent as a leader.

It did not hurt Reagan a bit, that he possessed the ability to deliver a speech and have a great presidential persona on television, and at public appearances, but the meat and potatoes of his presidency was that of the success and empowerment of his staff, simply put – "his leadership abilities".

If you wish to be a leader that knows how to think outside of the box, you must trust the intelligence and worth of the thought process of your staff, but not be unaware of the value of their mistakes or their actions. Try asking a staff member what you can do today for them to make themselves, or their ideas more effective within their daily plans, or the task they are required to perform.

Then stand back and watch the barriers of "can't" disappear before your very eyes. You will stand in absolute amazement, more times than not, at the solutions to problems and progress of the plan, as victory manifests itself as you clear the way, merely by endorsing and supporting their thoughts and actions.

By the way, any thought that just because you are the leader, you are suppose to know everything all of the time is nuts. They may have one idea, maybe one, but it was probably wrong, as to how to accomplish what you had asked them to do. But the empowered staff rarely disappoints the empowering leader.

The skill required to finding the value of a staff is not to limit the employees that follow you by being only as good, or as bright as you are, but to be as bright and intelligent as they possibly already are.

It was said of a team once, that there are ones in the team that were smarter than others on the team, but no one was smarter than the whole of the team. This is relevant only if the entire team is used, and the total of the group's intellect is recognized and encouraged.

Humility in leadership is one of the strongest tools of the leader. Remember "Humble, not stupid". Encouragement, empowerment, and the passionate belief in the people you have surrounded yourself with.

Your staff is the single key to the lock, and in many cases, to the very dungeon that imprisons the success you seek.

However, one must realize when they are in a box, or prison of self-centered thought, before one can come out, or break free again requires self-analysis and the honest, non-prejudicial appraisal of others.

8. To achieve an environment that endorses it's OK to say, "I don't know, but, as a TEAM, we'll find out."

It amazes me the depth and the extremes a person will go to, not to admit they don't know what they are doing. The main course on the menu of self-defeat is to be negative regarding every good, productive idea that is brought up. This method requires those that are empowered to prove their course of action to the naysayer thereby forcing someone to give all of the reasons why something should be done, or not done, without interactive communication. In the course of the sales pitch to overcome the obstacles placed before them, the negative approach, used by those that are suppose to know what they are doing, yet clearly do not have a clue, renders this negative method, as training to those that pretend to know what they are doing but actually don't.

As a leader, you must create an environment that encourages the admission of inability, or the lack of knowledge to perform the duties, or responsibilities at hand. A good employee that has held down a job for years, that has lost their way, or has lost their edge in the market, cannot easily admit they have lost their ability to stay up with the crowd, or to perform to the level of the young, hard charger.

This valued employee attempts to use seniority and/or founding father tactics, to hide behind their self-imposed grandeur and to use it as a defense mechanism to hold off the self admission that time has had its way with them and that they can no longer hold their own, when compared with the drive and energy of youth.

Most often for those in this seniority position, the historical tactics they have employed to win a war have become ineffective as a direct result of changing times and new technologies; however, again, due to rank and title, everyone assumes they know everything. They don't and you as a leader have probably created an environment that makes it impossible to say, "I Don't Know".

No one wants to admit what he or she can't do, or their tricks of the trade don't work as a result of their age, or a result of the inability to adapt to new techniques; again, especially when everybody assumes this person knows everything due to their seniority, rank, title or prestige.

A true empowering leader counts on age and/or length of service as wise counsel and creates an environment that allows, even encourages, anyone and everyone to make honest self-appraisals, without fear of looking dumb or ineffective.

As a society we tend to pass over the weak and the slow, however, continual analysis is required, as well as the environments you have built for people to work within, regardless of age, rank or title. As a leader you must do this before you can expect any admission from anyone, to anything, as to what they are not good at doing, or what they have counted on in the past that is now ineffective. What you can count on is them hiding behind past glories and victories or appearing to be arrogant when they actually are not.

Leaders, worth their weight, reward the honesty of the self-appraisals of an individual's abilities and inabilities, by the individual themselves. Ask your self as you review the employees: Have I reviewed the plan or the mission and their individual role and talent within it?

How can you expect anyone to grow and find solutions to problems in areas that the leader is truly not as gifted, or as trained, if the learning process stops as a result of fear?

As a potential result, if they admit they don't know something, based solely on everyone's assumption of their knowledge, they will lose their sense of worth to the team, and worse yet, to themselves. It is a direct hit on one's self-esteem. It would be like waking up in the morning and saying, "I can't wait to get to work and destroy my self-worth and be paraded, in disgrace, amongst my co-workers as a fraud".

The environment that encourages honest evaluations of talents and natural god-given gifts through self-analysis, without fear of retribution or humiliation, is a breeding ground for ordinary people to do extraordinary things.

The characteristics of a leader are vast. One common feeling among effective, team building leaders is the honest feeling after reviewing the challenges of their day; they feel they are so dumb they don't even know what they don't know.

Effective leaders constantly challenge every action and inaction to its ultimate worth and embrace each and every talent afforded to them through, and by, their team. An empowering leader must create a safe environment for honest appraisals of self, and of the team as a whole, in order to move the team toward the desired target.

9. To execute, based not on where we have been, but where we "CHOOSE" to go.

Through your actions, leadership, preparations, and empowerment you choose where you will go and to what level of success you will achieve. To look and live in yesterday, not accepting the fact that resistance, or reluctance to change in the marketplace, change within the battlefield, or change within yourself, spells out the odds for your success. The odds are very, very slim. To ignore, resist, or to refuse to change, is to die.

You choose where you go and what you will achieve; you are the one that chooses, no one else. Looking at history is very important, but more so is what not to do, in lieu of what to do. You have empowered your subordinates by telling them more of what they are doing right, so apply this principle to yourself as a leader. Remind yourself constantly of the things you do right but learn without ceasing, the things you did wrong, by an honest observation of yourself, your motives and your strategies, that yielded you the negative results. Do this, not as an emotional exercise, although it may become just that; but instead look at the history of your own actions, the strategies and tactics you selected, both individually, and as that of a leader, you will find the answers. Before you will lie the examples to avoid repeating previous failures and set an example for others to follow.

Reminds me of a senior executive that was interviewing for a CEO position with the Board of Directors. The candidate was asked what made him feel like he was qualified for the job, almost in an apologetic fashion, considering the candidates vast history in the industry and general business knowledge. The candidate thanked the interviewers for the opportunity to answer such a question and he replied, "gentlemen, you may think I am very smart, some may think that I learned what I know at the numerous educational intuitions I have attended, but frankly, the truth is, I have had to screw up a lot of companies to get this smart". It really helps to know hat not do sometimes, instead of what to do.

Positive possibilities should be based solely on desired outcomes, not on the foundational dwelling or the focusing on what we can't do. All of which should be based on learning from the past through the company's historical data, market actions, or through honest analysis of the company. As in "Alice and Wonderland" and the advice Alice was given, "it doesn't matter which direction you go, if you don't have a destination in mind, of where you wish to go".

Knowing where you want to go has to be matched to what, or where, you, or your company, has been and now chooses to go, short term and long term. Thereby, the actions of individuals, and the company as a whole can be evaluated as to the progress in reaching the chosen destination.

More times than not, empowerment problems, with both individuals and companies, deliberately deflect both from a straight, successful path to a desired target. A person can hurt the mission of the company, by any number of actions, just as the company's mission can dilute, or ignore, the talents of a person. It is a two way street.

As a leader, dwelling on the sins, or bad decisions of the past, it takes just as much energy placing one foot in front of the other, heading decisively to the desired goal, as it does to do nothing and stand still, dwelling on the mistakes of yesterday. Yesterday was yesterday and should serve as a positive reinforcement of your daily actions, not as a crutch, or an alibi, based on what not to do and on what to do. These moments are extremely powerful and require the company to reflect on all the things it has done right so that they do not to yield the same negative outcome as in the past.

The recognition of these remembrances become small power points that will confirm your drive to change the outcome, and to reach the goal that you have set.

Know where you are going and what the desired outcome is. Write it down and post it everywhere you can see it, right up under your nose, in an effort to remind you of where you have chosen to go.

I heard a joke once, that former First Lady, Barbara Bush, used in a speech to a group of students at Harvard University, regarding a that woman had prayed, seeking assistance, to become a better person.

Her prayer to God went like this:

"Dear God, I am trying so hard to be a better person. I have not gossiped all day, or spoken badly of anyone. I have tried so hard to think of the good in everyone and find the things in my life that I can change to make me a better person, and realizing the things I can't change. God I have concentrated on my confidence, not on self-anointed arrogance, and to attack this day to make something happen, positively, in my life, and in those that I know and work with. God, Thank you for you blessings and your patience with me, as I try to be the person you want me to be and to recognize the gifts you have given me. God, I know I could go on and on, but right now, I need to get out of bed, get dressed and get to work…and…I will…"

None of us wake up and say, "I think I will go to work today and cause a huge mistake. One so bad, that it will cost the company money, hurt someone, or maybe, I think I will go to work and dwell on the screw ups and bad decisions of the my past, and the company's past".

We run into the same problems, day after day, sometimes so spread out in their repetition, their appearance and in their recognition, that we don't connect the dots, in order to see the image and the actual cause of these problems and recognize the situations that may be self-induced. Although camouflaged by repetition we more than not, have the same response to the same problems time after time.

When reviewing a response, and only after one recognizes the problem as a potentially repeated situation due partly to our lack of response to it, you must look at your response, in direct relation to the choice that you made and the desired outcome. This must be done while reviewing the entire strategy you have chosen to employ. The problem, or situation must be fully faced, immediately, as an opportunity to use the situation to add to the positive employment of acts, or actions, that add to the results and completion of the overall mission.

To ignore an action, that fully embraces the freshly, discovered detour from the strategic path, is to add to the methodical derailment of the plan.

When you become or when you are made aware of the set of circumstances or bad decisions that keep you from the desired chosen outcome, if you ignore them, they become larger and more destructive than the tactics you use upon them, thereby, giving them more power by simply ignoring them.

Simple recognition of a problem, at the very least, gives you the chance to honestly decide and conclude a proper action, or actions, to correct it.

Ignoring, choosing not to address them, could be a conscious action, if they are immediately addressed and placed within the scope of the actions, or non-actions required. Then you can take a positive proactive position over the problem that faces you, and you can move on to the next challenge.

You can also place too much emphasis on the things you should ignore. It can be as simple as, **"Majoring in Minors"**. Letting the little things take a dominate position in your thoughts and actions leaving you with the feeling you are not getting anything done or you're not getting any closer to the target defined within the strategy. These obstacles are mostly self-induced through procrastination, thinking, or acting, as though if the problem is ignored, the problem, or situation, will just go away.

Although time does heal a lot of ills, knowing the difference between what the passing of time will heal and what screams for direct action is the balancing act required of an effective leader.

Choose your actions, and responses carefully, never ignoring the obvious, or put off facing a hard decision, or abusive situation, regardless how insignificant it can appear.

Remember, that the devil is in the details; also that no action is an action. You may implement a non-action through a well thought out process, analyzing the problem and greeting the problem at hand, as an opportunity of action, instead of ignoring that the problem even exist.

Focus on the chosen path to the target, not completely on where you have been or what you have done. I did not say, don't learn from your mistakes, but instead, focus on behavior, or spontaneous actions, that lead you to the desired outcome using the past as a map, as a real tool, for what you employ as a strategy, or tactic and for what success you expect to receive.

10.   Retain and protect our single greatest asset – each other, our personal self worth and the value of our brand equity.

The single greatest asset that we have is what we have in each other. To learn from, enjoy, and appreciate, the total of another's self worth, is immeasurable. If we could only recognize, and realize another's self worth and doing this we will find our own.

I can remember once after I left a company I found out that one of my largest customers had elected to change to a competitor's product, which in my opinion was inferior in comparison to what I had sold them. When I saw the President of this company at a trade show I ask why he had changed to a competitor's product from what I had sold him. His response surprised me. He advised me that although the product I sold him, clearly was far superior my old product had lost one of its key features to the competitive product. Startled and a bit confused at his answer I told him I understood but I was not aware of any changes my old company had made to the product. He responded by saying they had lost a major feature of the product, the salesman - me! That blew me away.

I was truly flattered and amazed at my own worth to the features of the product. We had spent hours upon hours in engineering, and in component reviews, to insure that our product was absolutely the best, feature by feature, part by part, yielding a premium price and a representative value for the product yet I had totally undervalued my own worth to the product.

When we realize that people buy from people, we start to understand the value of our own contributions, in relationships and actions, as it is related to the worth of a product. We all know this simple fact yet we spend very little of our resources to build upon the human features that delivers the goods.

Although, I must admit his answer could have given me an opportunity to feed my personal ego a t-bone steak, I elected to put his response in proper perspective, and remember, there is a fine line between confidence and arrogance.

All of us can be a feature of the product. I have always believed that **"Quality People build Quality Products"**. Now I understood a new dimension of our self-worth as a team, **"Quality People build, represent, and sell, Quality Products"**.

I had always known this, even assumed everyone else did as well but as most companies reviewing the buying and selling process, we spent our time, thoughts and energies trying to understand what the customer wants in products and services and giving it to them.

We labor over issues of price, reliability, timely deliveries and everything else under the sun yet we spend little time realizing that we, ourselves, and the things that we believe in and the things that we represent, as human beings, are also a central feature of the products we sell. It is not only the products individual integrity, or the depth of our services, but it is also the integrity and value of ourselves, as a people.

Brand Equity is not only the perceived and real value of the product but is also the recognized value, and perceptions of ourselves, how we think and who we are, as a people. Our approach, our actions, and even our beliefs, while addressing the needs, characteristics and requirements of a particular market or industry, are equally observed, measured and judged.

Chapter Nine

The Christmas Story – Pieces and Parts

In summary of these jewels of leadership, brings to mind a change in management, to some those two words represent an oxymoron. I am reminded of a story that involved a child that wanted a bicycle for Christmas and his Dad.

Once, during Christmas time, a little boy making his way to the local mall with his Dad to submit his Christmas wishes to Santa, told Santa, almost pleading, of his desire for a big boy bicycle. He had outgrown the tri-cycle and youth model bikes he had learned to ride on and wanted a bigger bike like the other kids on his block. Santa listened intently, as Dad paid close attention, as if he really had to since all he had heard from his Son for the last month was his desire for a Big Boy's Bike, gave the child a Peppermint stick and got the traditional Santa photo made.

On Christmas eve, as the child slept, the Dad being a great Dad, and one of Santa's elves as well, and after buying the bike days earlier, addressed the task of putting it together at the last minute, as Christmas, as usual, had been a hectic time with his Son at home for the Christmas holidays. All Dads know that that putting together swing sets, bikes, tricycles, is not the easiest task in the world, after enjoying the events of Christmas eve with family and friends, then having to face the book of instructions and looking for the proper tools in the wee hours of Christmas morning. All Dads know this drill

You take all the parts out, survey the assorted nuts and bolts, wheels, seat, frame, handle bars and think to them selves, this can't be that hard. Relying on their childhood memories of taking apart, and putting back together, their own bike, hundreds of times while growing up, starts putting wheels on, seats, chains, handlebars, etc. But, he realizes that he does not have the tools he needs to tighten up all the nuts and bolts, nor does he have the one, or two, wrenches he actually needs, which is in some painfully dark toolbox in car trunk or garage. More than likely he sits their in his stocking feet, most likely dressed for bed, thinking to himself, and being a lot tired and a little lazy to get dressed to go on a searching mission for the proper tools, elects to finger-tighten all the nuts and bolts, so it looks like a bike, and justifies his laziness by thinking to himself, it will be put together for his Son's Christmas morning, but together they can tighten all the nuts and bolts, as Father/Son thing Christmas morning.

The Dad finally gets to bed and sleeps soundly. Until he hears the screams of delight proclaiming that Santa brought him a bike. The Father sleepily drags himself from the bed to enjoy, his son's joy seeing his new "Big Boy Bike".

The father explained that Santa did not have time to tighten up all the bolts and for the son to wait just a minute before the son took it outside to ride it. While the child didn't care if he was in his PJs, Dad had to go up stairs, hurried, get dressed and then gather up the tools needed to tighten up all the nuts and bolts. The Father hurried upstairs to replace his nightclothes for some suitable for the neighborhood, but while Dad was changing the son took the bike out and commenced to climb aboard and ride it.

Needless to say as the boy mounted the bike and attempted to ride it, the bike fell apart, pieces and parts flying everywhere. Wheels were in bushes, handlebars landed across the street and the frame hung around the boy's neck like a 40-pound necklace.

Sobbing pitifully the boy destroyed in heart, knowing he had ruined his prize possession. The father, after checking to see that his son was ok, other than the boy having a bruised and broken heart, began to explain to his son what had happened.

"Son, I told you to wait on me, we had to tighten up all the nuts and bolts. All the pieces were there when you found your bike under to tree, and they were in the right places, it looked like a bike, smelled like a bike, but is wasn't a bike in function, not until we tightened all the parts in their proper places. Then it would become a bike in form, fit and function.

There is a business moral within this story.

As we organize pieces and parts of our organizations, companies, even departments, the pieces not only have to be in their proper place but also they must be tightened down where all the pieces and parts can work together for the whole, to act as one, for one common purpose or objective. Each piece is equally important, one not more or less important than the other. The leader is the Dad that must maintain control that the customer, or the one the company exist for, does not attempt to use what it is not; and the leader must tighten down each part, one to another, to fit the purpose of the end result intended.

In so many companies arrogance or egos enters with a vengeance, urging one department to say or feel that they are more important that the other. You know how it goes around the office, "sales is more important than finance", "operations is more important than sales", "executive management is more important than anybody". None are true, and none of the departments, or people are more important than the whole of the company and the mission it has undertaken.

This sounds simple, almost elementary; in fact, it is, yet still in today's workplace the posturing for departmental, or employee dominance, one over the other remains a crippling disease that robs a company of it's talent, it's efficiency, and even it's worth. This is not contradictory to the idea of the individual rising to the level of their own personal excellence, but offers a challenge to today's leader to empower all within the organization and putting people in the right jobs at the right time and bringing up the performance level of the whole company at once. It is possible, and hard, but very productive, and ultimately profitable.

There is another roadblock that interferes with putting things in their perspective place similar to the bicycle, yet this one deals with the revered Tradition of a company. You know, "that is the way we have always done it", "we don't do things like that around here", "we are just a small company, we can't do things like the big guys do". (There's that word again – CAN'T)

"Tradition" is one of the worse diseases known to the business world. It breeds compliancy and in-efficiencies.

To make a point, once an electronics company, in which I was familiar with, and had been run by several different owners through changing times and Lord knows what else, had gone into receivership and had been acquired by a similar firm in another part of the country. The buyers were also an old, establish company, and were similar in many ways. The acquiring company's saving grace was a series of patents and unmistakable manufacturing efficiencies that had held them up, and supported them through the changing times and economic downturns. However, the acquired firm was not so lucky nor, became apparent as agile to change to the market and manufacturing processes.

After acquiring the company, the buyers, knowing all the people in the company they had bought because they were in a similar industry, just left the managers in charge, all of them, the executive staff, the middle managers and all of the support personnel.

Things rocked along, with business as usual, nothing changed, except the name on the bottom of everyone's paycheck and increased payables beyond where the company had been when it went into receivership. The business continued to get worse and worse, yet for whatever reason, it was left alone, without any corporate intervention. The acquition was causing tremendous drain on the cash flow of the acquiring company and its primary core business at its primary location. Enough was enough and there was a general house cleaning. A new corporate exec arrived and cut workforce trying to find a place to hang on financially while he re-organized the manufacturing operation and tried to find out what in the heck was happening. Orders were down, profit per product was non-existent, quality was awful, and employee moral was lower than a snake's belly in a wagon rut.

The new exec found that there was a manufacturing management process of "hit or miss", based on the way plants worked 20 years ago and inventories and manufacturing processes and computer driven controls and manufacturing key indicators were not to be found.

Change was in order immediately, but the demon called "Tradition" reared it's ugly head. Every time processes were changed and the boys from "Corporate" left town, things went right back to where they were. Lip service, to the boys at the new corporate office, was the battle cry of those entrenched in their denial for a need to change. "The way we worked has always worked before", was recited over and over again by the old company's employees. The new exec returned after putting the old guys in new jobs, after being told the old, yet newly installed managers, understood their mission of change.

After about two months of continuing losses, it had gotten to the point of closing down the factory. The exec returned and fired all the people that he had put in charge of change, and at the same time, fired the entire executive staff, middle management and support staff, and then rehired most of them, after interviewing them, one at a time for different positions, than the ones they held before in most cases. Only about 20 percent of the fired management employees were hired back into their old jobs.

When ask by one of the plant workers what took corporate so long to make these changes. They thought the acquiring company would have made these kinds of changes to begin with, since those were the same guys that ran the company to bankruptcy.

The exec knew that the hardest demon to kill is that called "Tradition". The only way was to kill the beast and let it rot and start smelling really bad where the employees would beg corporate to please come bury it and get the rotting carcass out of the front yard, so to speak.

The acquiring company had tried to let the original executive management turn it around, and make it profitable, believing the previous owners were to blame for the poor performance. But in fact, it was "Tradition", along with changing economic times that the company was not able to stay up with manufacturing efficiencies and quality, by doing things," The way they always did it". The electronics industry is hard enough as it is and as rapid the pace of electronics technology, all of the employees wrote their company's epitaph, "Killed by Tradition".

Tradition defeated the British; those Redcoats made a fine target for the guys laying in the ditch with their squirrel gun's.

It is unfortunate, that when you shoot a critter in your front yard, 'cause it keeps digging holes in your yard, you have to let it rot and stink to high heaven, and then, and only then, due to the occupants, living in your house and due to their allegiance to their so-called "Tradition" of not wanting to shoot the critter, they will not let you bury it, they just want to pretend it is not there, because they don't want anyone to know they would do such a thing. You have to let it stink, rot and decompose, stink up the entire world before the occupants in your house beg you to bury it, when they could have buried it anytime they wanted to; but "Tradition" and what other people think prevented that from happening. The smell had to get bad enough for someone, now everyone helping to go find a shovel and participate in the burial. This a lot like changing an old family- owned, established, passed down company.

This method of change is truly the most expensive, both financially and emotionally, yet when "Tradition" is in it's full fury, sometimes the only way to get the workers to want the old ways to die and to be permanently buried, and find a place to start over is to let them all die…and get to stinking.

The company is now doing quite well. Managers have learned their new jobs, empowerment abounds, solutions flowing from the bottom up, not driven down by corporate management or self-centered directives, encouragement of each other is the norm and the future of the company and it's profits and sales are bright, as the people have their livelihood, and have regained their self-esteem.

Chapter Ten

Welcome to the Land of "Can"

"Can't never did nothing", as my Mama used to say. The sheer fact that enthusiasm and passion can melt away doubt and negative responses and attitudes in all that come in contact with the mighty weapon, called enthusiasm and will. She also told me to never pass up a good fight without gettin' in it. I have resisted this advise in my older years, nor have I passed it on to my children.

It has been studied, by the medical community, that being subjected to a steady dose of positive, motivational messages, has a positive effect on your health, by releasing endorphins into your blood stream, thereby producing a sense of well being, and creating a definite improvement in your general health at large.

Endorphins produce the same effect to your body as a "runners high" or, on a culinary observation, the same effects as eating a bag of Red Peppers, which I do not suggest, regardless of your need for motivation. I can assure you, you would be motivated, if you were to do the later; motivated, at least, to find some ice water or respond with some other normal bodily function.

The need to have an attitude of winning is absolutely required, to face the negatives, and the objections that are encountered routinely, through the forces of fear, apathy and disempowerment. This mindset of "can", or any proactive possibility, produces a pattern of thought that will exhaust every possible strategy, and /or solution to the mission and obstacle you are facing.

As a warrior on the field of battle, the warrior does not raise his sword, in the belief that he will perish for if this were his thought his sword would never leave its scabbard, he would just accept death, not attempting to even run for his life. His enemy would merely take out his sword and slay him or should I say he would have slain himself, defeated before the battle even began.

The commands, or goals given by leaders, such as the commands of a field general, must be seen as possible and probable in order to unite his soldiers in a common mission of war; all the while painting a vision of success and planning the expected result, for they're placing themselves in peril, or in harms way.

I assure you the idea of losing a war, or dying in the field of battle might be admitted as a risk of war, but I assure you, no general, in true command, ever told or acknowledged, or spoke of failure, while addressing his troops before the dawn of the battle.

Although a good leader acknowledges that fear is understandable and normal. To embrace fear as a reason for why he or his troops cannot complete their mission or win their war, is unthinkable and foreign to the passion of man and mission.

The word "can" exists where hope meets purpose. The possibilities of a positive, passionately, poised plan is infinite. The word "can" is the weapon of the warrior that fails to quit, regardless of his fear or his inability; for to quit is to lose, to lose is to die. The word "can", much the same as in the way the sword was built, the fires of the furnace must temper ones dedication to the plan.

One must take the plan of "can" unto themselves, it must become one with the warrior's mind and spirit and must process an edge that is unyieldingly sharp, in order to split the dulling truths of defeat, without surrender to the idea of "can't" and to fight again, and again, until victory, or the completion of plan is realized.

The warrior's sword must be kept sharp. As it slices through objection after objection, negative after negative, defeat after defeat, because the edge, naturally, becomes dull. The warrior's inter-strength of resolve and his mission to complete his task must be balanced with an effort to be one with his sword and to keep its edge sharp and deadly.

The determination to win and to hold dear, deep in his heart, the word "can", keeping the passions, and the fires of the plan alive. This commitment keeps the edge on the sword, putting to death any enemy that may rise against it until victory is gained.

In the days of the ancient warrior, a warrior's weapon was his sword, very similar to the tactics and strategies we employ today. To speak of the sword romantically, it was one of a partnership, trusting ones own life and the lives of the others that you pledged to protect. As is a plan, or strategy, one must become one with it. A leader must become the plan, the strategy, and the mission - to have the passion of heart to complete the goals that lie before him, never calling for retreat.

As for the sword, it is only a piece of steel, yet so unmistakably alive to the touch, waiting and able to magically bestow, and insert the power of its temper, its fire, its strength, into the hands that hold it. For within the magic of its movement, to be seen and poetically felt, as if to be a timeless symbol of both peace and war, of both good and evil, is to be so beautifully revealed and seen so honestly, of bravery and of cowardice, of strength and of weakness, of victory, and of defeat.

The acts of your day are the swings of your sword. Your attempt to fight, struggle and to beat the demons of life that stand before you, your daily actions are the strategies of your sword's cut, the depth of your thrust and the edge you have placed upon its blade. For the blade of the sword of the successful warrior, is sharpened by the heat of humility and the fires of honesty.

For as God purchased his children with the most powerful of all weapons, the sword of forgiveness, the sword of honesty is the edge that grinds away at the enemies armor, leaving them unable to fight, much less, able stand in the light of day. For honesty in your actions and the actions of your honesty are invincible. Be one with the sword.

Excepts from **"The Sword"**, by Rod Richardson

"Its' fluid and flowing movements,

its' shining brilliance against the sky,

its' very being miraculously

and passionately employed

from the spirit

and the mind of its' holder;

Born from the fires

that made it strong

and gave it its' perfect

and pure heat of honesty.

For the sword will never die...

Death comes only

to the one that stands before it

or behind it...

be one with the sword".

To merely take this sword into your hands, is to be consecrated as a union of one, of one mind, and of one heart; to defy, to protect, to attack, to carryout, to conquer, to spill and employ the whole of one's self, unto the unforgiving dispatch of the wars of will and, likewise, the wills of war.

To seek the sword, is the undeniable surrender of one's self, to be transported into the fires of the furnace from which the sword came, making the hopeful assumption, proclaiming that you too, can withstand the heat of the fire, and the strike of the hammer, as to have earned, and to use the strength of its' temper.

"Welcome to the Land of Can"

"Oh for the field of battle. The fear, the courage, the hope, the honesty of heart, the welling up of pure humility, coupled with the resolve of a thousand fearless and loyal warriors, standing before and behind you. The smell of your own blood, yet to be spilled, in a joyful release of pure and passionate determination to survive and

empower. Yet with sadness, for the lost and misled spirits that you have slain, and the poor souls that will forever long for their slain, and for their disgusting memory. For they could never to be mourned or missed, more than I will miss them, for what they could have been, or what they could have contributed to their fellow man. Yet, lost, restored, or decisively destroyed...all will be judged, on and after the field of Battle!

Sad you may think; Sad, that fear and hopelessness disappears in a sea of unbridled joy of purpose and rebirth? How sad is it? It's NOT! It is only battle, as if the word "only" could ever be spoken in the same breath, as the word" battle".

Smell and taste the fallen evil as it lies before you, joyfully broken, disembodied, without power!

Touch...Feel the power, a personal power that has been released into the children of the victor.

For it is as real today, as it was in Ancient Rome, Gladiators we are all, to fight for the Kingdom and the Glory of a place called CAN!"

Chapter Eleven

What Does a leader look like?

I am constantly amazed at the presumption of what a leader is supposed to look, dress, act, or behave like. Though race, creed, and color have been addressed, and without exception to gender and expectations of appearance, a leader's looks continue to be addressed through the perceptions of, and by the troops that follow them. This expected appearance, which is of a particular mindset, or of the collective opinion by peer management, it is not the same, nor is it the same held by the executive management in which a leader may report to or the stockholders and constituents they serve. So tell me, just what exactly does a leader look like?

That's simple - just go look in the mirror, if you dare. Behind and within the image you see, is a leader. Not from appearance, nor through race, creed or color, nor gender, but through daily actions, beliefs, passion, and ultimate commitment; and above all, results and contributions.

Which brings me to an opinion on "women in leadership". Women are the truest of all warriors, and some of the most effective and powerful leaders in the world or its history.

The women of war, those that carry the sword of leadership in full combat, not by design but by a passion for justice, and a rage for the dishonesty and the cowardice of man in battle. Not to resent, nor needing to give any recognition to the self-anointing command of man, by man; but to arise and take up the sword of battle, and lead the very fruits of their wombs; to give leadership to the wandering and lost purpose of man.

These women of war do not have to be given titles or positions of rank, for in full battle, they have already been given them for they were earned. For those of male gender wearing the armor of war, whom adorned by their own arrogance, should fear the power of this female Gladiator. It is a deadly mistake to take lightly, or to disbelieve, the power of this warrior with genderless sword.

Tell me, oh brave and noble warrior, of the feel of the full cut and strength of her sword, as you die. Tell me my powerful, superior male warrior, was the sword of your death male, or was it female? Women's strength and intelligence, their minds of pure and purposeful, compassionate leadership, their controlled command of leadership is god-given not as that of man's ordination, which is self appointed, by and of, himself.

No, Leaders are not anointed they must endure the test of battle. These women of war are born, created by God, installed and called to embrace, endure, edify the truest qualities of leadership, both God- given and deserved, they lead the lost and the brave in battle.

God help, and have pity on, the fools of battle that face the decisive sword of a woman, in and of full command, and of leadership. Their cut is deep and forever, merciful, yet deliberate, without regret, without remorse, as they slay the stupidity and arrogance of man on and off the field of Battle.

These women of war are the warriors that fight by the side of man and deservedly have earned their rightful place in leadership. It is a pity that man cannot betray his prejudice long enough to recognize their character without comments of gender, without ignorance, but with the same taste for justice as does the female leader; a justice that flavors the fruits of the battle, a battle that knows not gender, yet respects only the results and contributions of the victor.

Choose if you must, in your mind, what a leader looks like. For a leader is not defined by race, creed, color, religion, gender, education, country-club membership, or those born into the "Lucky Kid Club", those born with a silver spoon in their mouth. Leaders are the ones that have vision and purpose to empower the masses, leading those begging for direction within the whole of the group and within themselves.

Chapter Twelve

"Lead...Follow...or get thy worthless self behind me"!

Praise God for an example of leadership or salesmanship, which, we can follow. The greatest salesman of eternity, Jesus Christ, a salesman that sold something that could not be touched, sold or seen, all for the mere price of your entire life!

To betray self and exist for the glory, and in complete servitude to God and to God's children, to be a servant, to be a leader from the knees up, to embrace being the lowest, in order to obtain the highest, that is the true meaning of the word, "leader".

A leader, a CEO, COO, CFO, President, or any types of executive manager, empower those you believe to be strong for the strong also need to be led. Lead and empower those who appear to be weak and without hope, for they will lead you to courage and your own humility. Lead, daily, those that will follow, as they make their personal journey beyond the tangled intelligence of man and the desperate hope to contribute within a world of a lost and searching humanity.

Be grateful for those with soaring souls with the trusting hope of a child. Embrace these people, these children of God, God's property knowing or not, they belong to God; they are gifts to each of us from God. They are those with an honest heart and an undeniable claim for a better future.

God Bless the Children! Be as one. Why can we not see each other as a child does; trusting, full of hope, without prejudice, worthy of the bounty of heaven and earth?

No greater gift can a man leave to this earth, than the hearts, souls, and dreams of his own children. The gift of a child's trust is the only thing in this world that is true and is worth attempting to understand as we fight and struggle with the task of leadership. For children are the true example of leadership – trust, hope and un-selfishness, unconditional love for those they may not understand, and for those that may not understand them.

I will ask it again, is the burden of leadership heavy? Only to the one that tries to carry "self" along for the journey!

Remember, leadership requires an eye on the possible, while struggling with feet buried in the earthly reality of lost hope and the relentless screams of dismay and the loss of heart, while fighting, struggling, to free the souls and the talents, hopes and dreams of the scattered and scorned.

Again, for unto thee, I continue to say…

"Leaders are not anointed…they emerge from within the blood, sweat and fear of battle, not through rank or title, nor draped in arrogance or ego…but in quiet confidence, to expend the sum of their life's experience, talents, skills and God-given blessings toward the battle at hand, without regard for self, but with total regard for the success of the whole."

How can one explain the characteristics and the worth of the empowering leader, a leader with a plan, a leader that is one within the plan, with the people, with God as his Master, a leader right down to the fiber of his very body, it all boils down to five words, "Selfless, Fearless, Humble, Honest, Priceless…**Leaders, Arise…empower…contribute and seek the rewards of the greatest gift of all, "a servant's heart in a King's clothes".**

There is actually only one "How To" book on Leadership. You really don't have to look that hard for it. You can find it in any bookstore. It is called the "Bible", the one and only, holy and divine, "How To" manual on "Leadership". Read it…**I dare you.** Ask these questions of your employees…try it. "What can I do for you today to make your day more effective and more enjoyable?", "How can I help you accomplish and realize you goals?" **Thanks for reading this book...I pray that you will accept all of the gifts God has designed just for you, the ones inside of you and the ones that are sitting next to you...*May God Bless you richly in the name of our Savior, Jesus Christ.***

About the Author

Rod has been well versed in executive corporate leadership. His lessons and examples of business leadership defy common corporate tradition and he focuses on methods to get the best out of the organization. His writing brings many unorthodox experiences to bear such as being a professional trainer of competitive and ranch quarter horses for 20 years and being a key executive in the heavy duty automotive industry of some of this county's largest corporations. Rod holds a MBA and a PhD and uses a prose technique that requires you to go to a place within yourself.